Brenda Martin Schurr

ONLY FIVE YEARS

Love, Separation, Loss, Acceptance

In Memory of Steven Wayne Martin, Captain, U.S.M.C. 1943~1968

Only Five Years

Copyright © 2020 by Brenda Martin Schulz.

Cover Design by 100Covers.com
Interior Design by FormattedBooks.com

ISBN   978-1-7345810-03

History swirls around him as

his story is told

and his dreams are altered by
the continuing escalation
and American involvement
in the Vietnam War.

REVIEWS

I greatly admire the determination and tenacity of my life-long friend, Brenda Schulz, the author of "Only Five Years." She was my best friend in high school. She displays courage and conviction in revealing the tender part of her young life. The letters between Brenda and the Captain tell a good deal about America in the 1960's.

The dynamics of Brenda's family life are intriguing. Her marriage to the first love of her life, and the close bond she formed with her young husband's family, enabled her to liberate herself from the stifling environment in which she grew up. The life changing experiences in which she finds herself prepares Brenda to find her own identity and self-worth, and eventually, independence.

Elizabeth S. Keister, B.A. Psychology

Vietnam Veterans in particular, and even those who may have opposed the conflict, will love reading "Only Five Years." Captain Martin spares no details in letters to his new bride concerning the Marine Corps basic training, and in country Vietnam helicopter rescue and supply missions. He was adept at describing a foreign land and the daily grind and facts of life living in a war torn country. The correspondence between the Captain and his wife not only show tenderness, but reveal the couple's values and the beauty of young love. Readers will become aware of the striking contrast between the 1960's and the present day. "Only Five Years" is a journey the reader doesn't want to end.

Jane S. Walsh, M.Ed.

Contents

N

Foreword

N

It has been more than a half century since Captain Steven W. Martin, U.S. Marine Corp was a helicopter pilot in Vietnam. This is his story, and I am honored to introduce the friend I found as a teenager and the story of the man he became.

I was academically able and yet a little socially inept. That began to change when I boarded the school bus that first day of high school, when the teens in the back of the bus eyed me suspiciously, as I found a seat by myself.

Within minutes, Steve risked the driver's ire by slipping into the seat next to me and introduced himself. Steve may not have meant to overhaul my social life, but he began the process quickly! He introduced me to other kids and over the next weeks he and I became best friends.

He entertained me with tales of hunting and fishing in our woods and mountains of New Hampshire, and my education was rapid and daunting as my first attempt to fire a 12 gauge shotgun knocked me to the ground. The most basic element was that Steve Martin was a really neat guy with a treasure trove of experience and a manner through which I could learn of them.

After high school graduation I went to the Air Force Academy, and Steve went to college to pursue his interests in forestry and wildlife. One summer he said he hoped to become a Marine pilot since the war in Vietnam wasn't going away, and that is how he wished to serve. I doubt he ever knew how much that excited me! My forestry and wildlife buddy was going to be a combat pilot after college. This was much as I hoped I could be!

We were both focused on academics and finding "the girl." He found Brent and was much more focused earlier than I. Their romance is detailed in this book.

The last time I would see Steve was when he was in flight training in Pensacola, Florida, and I was also in flight training in Selma, Alabama. We met up in Pensacola and had a rolling, happy discussion of flight training and other trivia of the day.

A few years later, and before I could get checked into the new unit I was assigned to, I received the stunning news that Steve had been killed in a mid-air in Vietnam. Upon obtaining leave and on the flight home, I thought about the things we had done and the many more we intended to do over the years to come.

Brent had absorbed a lot of the training Steve had and was dignified and restrained throughout the service and interment of one of the greatest men I had ever known. Since that day I've thought about the loss I feel and the privilege it was to have known him and to learn from him. He was, and is, the hero in my life. Bless you, Captain Steven Wayne Martin, USMC.

Your Friend,
Peter Miner, Colonel USAF (Retired).

Introduction

N

Only Five Years is a story of reflection upon a journey of love, separation, loss, and acceptance. Although written about the world of one man and his family, it is a microcosm of all those and their families, who have served our country in war or peace time.

Captain Martin's letters and journal were not ordinary rhetoric, but a young man's viewpoint of the world he lived in. Upon considering requests for letters from Vietnam by collectors; and having known him and loved him, it was a story only Brent (His nickname for her.) could tell. His letters were love letters, but also a history of what was going on around him; and his outlook on life, achievement, love, family, loyalty, his country, war and duty. May this memoir honor the man that he was.

Chapter 1

The Chest Of Scary Things

Brent lifts the objects from the old cedar chest. A young man's voice speaks softly, "Ah, the chest of scary things," disclosing his memory of learning about its contents when he was a young child.

Mother and son respectfully handle the hats, the pictures, the Journal, the Flight Log, the awards and medals, the neatly folded American flag, and letters from a man he would never know, other than through the history of these objects.

This son was the one who, while working as a teacher in China, took his mother to the edge of the South China Sea, to look south to where the owner of these objects spent the last year of his life: Vietnam.

Brent began writing, organizing and sorting the letters, so her son might know the man. Though not his own father, this man's life and death were the shaping of his mother's life. She was ready to reveal the shattering of a family; and the resolve to carry on as he would have wanted.

Singers tell their story through songs. Artists through their colors. Steve and Brent now share their story in their own words from their letters and his Journal that covers a period of five years from their meeting in 1963 until his death in 1968. Their story is unique to one particular young couple from two small towns in New Hampshire, and yet their story is universal, reflective of young people around the world, torn between love and dreams, and a duty to their country during military conflicts. It was only five years. And yet the relationship would last forever.

THE CHEST OF SCARY THINGS

Where It All Began

S. W. MARTIN
104 EAST HALL
Durham, N.H.

#1!
1963 . 5/3

DURHAM, N.
MAY
8-AM
1963

Miss Brenda Chaney
to Tuftonboro, N.H.

R.F.D.

The First Letter

Chapter 2

Where It All Began, 1963

April 27, 1968. Brent was at the end of her senior year in high school. She was invited by her brother and his girlfriend for a weekend visit to the campus of their university in New Hampshire. It happened to be the weekend of the annual Sadie Hawkins Dance. She knew it was a dance where the girls get to ask the boys to dance, and it was a little intimidating to a not yet high school graduate.

In the crowd Brent noticed a tall, nice looking guy who was not actually dancing with anyone. He glanced at her and moved in her direction; but as she was working up her courage to ask if he wished to dance, he turned away from her as if to engage in conversation with someone else. Years later, to her amusement when thinking about their first meeting, that it was his "fake-out" and his assessment of her intentions! To Brent's great relief he turned towards her in the crowd, and she remembers mumbling something resembling an invitation to dance. Even though she doesn't remember the song that was playing, it was to be the dance that would be in her memory for the rest of her life.

As it turned out neither of them were very good dancers; and at his invitation, a walking tour of the campus provided a much better opportunity to actually talk. The first discovery was that they had grown up in neighboring towns, over an hour north of the university. He was finishing his second year of college, and she had plans to go to a three year nursing school in the fall. The evening ended with a walk back to the dorm where Brent was staying. And yes, there was a good-night kiss!

May 3, 1963: Dear Brent, I would like to thank you for a wonderful evening last Saturday. I really enjoyed meeting you and would like to see you again sometime. I hope that you had a good time also, and would you be willing to chance seeing me again; providing I promise not to go dancing.

Did you enjoy your look at the campus Saturday? It is one of the best-looking campuses in New England. I imagine your brother is looking forward to getting out as is everyone else.

All this week I've been wondering how I could get to see you again. To tell the truth, I've spent most of this last week building up my courage to write this letter. So, it all comes down to this. If you would like to go out some weekend in the near future (We could go bowling, movies, or something) would you drop me a line. If you'd like, we could even double with Rich and his girl. I'll let you know in plenty of time beforehand when I'll be home for a weekend, so that you can tell me whether you can or can't go out; if you have decided that you would like to go out with me.

Well, I had best close for now and hit the books for a few hours. Yours truly, Steve. May 5, 1963: Dear Steve, I was very surprised and delighted to receive your letter. I was on your campus Friday to see my brother graduate.

but, it seems our paths didn't cross that day. I enjoyed my two visits to the campus very much.

I am very glad you built up enough courage to write, and I wouldn't mind at all if you continued to do so. And yes, I would like to go out with you. Always, Brent.

May 12, 1963: Dear Brent, Sorry about the long silence that followed your letter. I had three exams this last week that I had to really study for. (I wasn't delaying seeing you!) By the time they were over I wasn't capable of adding two and two and coming up with the same answer twice. I hope I passed, but with me you can never tell.

I'm glad to hear you liked our campus; but, I was surprised to learn that this was your second visit. I hope you had a chance to really have some fun here.

Well, starting this week we have ten days of classes left. I suppose you are looking forward to the summer as much as we are. Pretty soon it will be graduation time for you, and another part of your life will be put behind you. I hope you will be able to look back on your high school days with the same feeling I have when I look back upon mine.

I will be home this weekend; and if it is alright with you, we could go bowling Friday night. If it would be better for you, we could make it Saturday; but, there is a little "if" of my own involved with Saturday night. I work Saturdays, and I never know when I'll be getting out of work. This last Saturday it was 8:30 that night. Something like that would give us an awfully late start. So, if you are willing to take the chance, drop me a line. If you don't want to change anything, I will pick you up around 7:30 Friday night. If you have something else planned, don't be a bit afraid to tell me so. Hope we can make connections this weekend. Steve. (P.S. You underrate yourself if you were really surprised to hear from me.)

How To Win A Girl's Heart

Chapter 3

How To Win A Girl's Heart

May 20, 1963: Dear Brent, I'm pleased to relate that you were a smash hit last Friday night at my home. Just to show you I was not talking through my hat, I had quite a time convincing one member of the family that you were a senior in high school and not a college girl.

I hope we didn't scare you too bad as we may be wild; but, we are really harmless. If you can stand me, you have survived the worst the Martin's have to offer. In fact, you made a hit all over. Charlie wanted to know all about you. Too bad my boss wasn't there. I might have gotten a raise in pay. I guess it pays to be seen with a good looking girl now and then. Steve.

June 3, 1963: Dear Brent, It seems like ages since I have seen those eyes of yours. This doesn't mean I can't imagine what they look like. I have seen the darn things every time I have sat down for a moment. (This does not make for very easy studying, so have pity on this poor simple fellow.) But every so often I like to see the real thing, just to prove to myself they are from this world.

Boy, I had better close before this turns into a real honest-to-God love letter. That would be something that would produce many a laugh by those who know me. Steve.

Arrangements were made for Steve to attend Brent's high school graduation, and she was thrilled when a dozen red roses were delivered to her home. Best of all, he was there for the graduation ceremony.

The summer months of June, July, and August of 1963 there was no need for letters between Steve and Brent. Living only thirteen miles distance from each other the writing was halted, and the real dating and solidifying of their relationship occurred. The tires on his parent's car had to have been worn down considerably that summer with all the travel back and forth; not to mention those of friends with whom they double dated.

Brent was delighted to be a frequent guest for dinners with his family and the joining in of the many evening swims in the lake by the house. Other dates included bowling, going to movies, and romantic walks in the country. Along with many hugs and kisses were the discussions about the future for them and things they would like to have in their future home. One thing Brent recalls was telling Steve she hoped they would always have ice cream in the refrigerator, and he was amenable to that! One thing they didn't agree on was that he wanted a gas stove in the kitchen, and she wanted an electric stove!

The summer ended, and by September Steve was back for his junior year at the university. Brent was starting a three year nursing program in another city. The letter writing was to start again in earnest.

September 9, 1963: Dearest Steve, Everything is going well, and I just finished my first day of classes! We had Anatomy & Physiology, Professional Adjustment, and Nursing Fundamentals for today. They are breaking us in easy it seems. Chemistry and Microbiology are to be introduced in a few days.

I will be able to go home this weekend. Classes will be done at 2:30, Friday afternoon. You don't suppose I could get a date with a good looking "potential" Marine for that night do you? If you know of such a person, I'd love to have him pick me up here whenever he could Friday afternoon. If you can't find such a person, let me know.

By Friday I will have a million things to tell you. Right now there isn't as much. I'd rather talk to you than write anyway. The sound of your voice is much nicer than the scratch of this pen!

Four of us girls went downtown this forenoon. Guess the locals know there is a new class of student nurses in town. We collected about five whistles, many stares, and a few car horn toots. Pretty bad I'd say. I'd much prefer to have the Martin wolf whistle.

The "Rules." I can't receive or make telephone calls after 10:00 p.m., unless it is an emergency. Study Hall every night except Friday, from 6:00 p.m. to 9:00 p.m., in one's own room. May visit with other students from 9:00 p.m. to 10:00 p.m.! Bedtime at 10:00 p.m. Until I see you again. Love, Brent.

N

This letter indicates Brent's acknowledgement of Steve's potentially becoming a United States Marine after his college graduation. Although, in thinking back, it didn't seem to be an actuality for her at that time.

The escalation of the Vietnam "War" was not far from the minds of and in the discussions of young men on college campuses around the country. Steven was proud of his father's service in the U.S. Army during World War II; and he had known early on that he would serve someday, if needed. Being a strong minded young man, he knew when the time came, that he would chose the branch of the service in which he would serve: The United States Marine Corps.

N

September 16, 1963: Dearest "Dr. Steve," I wish to consult with you for a cure for an acute heart condition. The symptoms are as follows: extreme sullenness, glazed stare, inability to study, craving to write letters to one person, and a dull pain in the thoracic cavity. Is there any known cure for such impossible symptoms? I'm sure a man of your outstanding ability can surely recommend something. The patient needs to consult with you Dr. Steve, at your convenience.

Letters and thoughts will prevent complications for the first week, and a trip home will put one a few miles closer. However, after a two week period the patient is sure to develop severe and serious complications; thus bringing the lacrimal glands and ducts into function. It seems that only a consultation with you Dr. Steve, will assuage a rise in the mortality rate. Please hurry to our aid as soon as possible. Signed: Nurse In Charge, Brent.

Hi Darling! Hope you like the above plea. I just had a good wave of missing you pass over me. You had better write and give me a good scolding, as I'm not supposed to spend study hours writing letters. I went downtown today and saw a store you shopped in occasionally. I just stood there and savored the fact that you had been there. With all my love, Brent.

September 1963: Dearest Brent. Nurse In Charge: As for your case, I suggest group therapy. The group should be fairly small, say two people, of course to be of any help the other person should feel the same. I have just the person for our little group. I feel they should be left alone to work out their problem by themselves. They must have the proper surroundings of course. I suggest a late movie, fireplace, and a nice fire and most important is to include the two people themselves. All the above are just suggestions; open to revision. One thing I hope you will agree with is that treatment begin at the earliest possible moment. Steve ("Dr. Steve")

September 18, 1968: Dearest Brent, It seems like ages since I heard the sound of your voice and your laughter. I miss being with my girl. It will be wonderful when I'm able to go home to her. It helps to know she is happy in what she is doing.

Coming back here was like coming home. It seems like I have never been away. I'm actually very lucky. It seems, when I think about it, that I have three homes: college where I spend most of my time, where my family is, and where my girl is. No matter where I am, I will always be close to one of these. I actually scare myself in my willingness "to have at it." It looks like a tough semester coming up, but only on the surface. I'm going to run all of my subjects right into the ground. This year I have everything pulling for me. I'm walking very proud. It is quite a feeling to be so sure (almost as strong as my feelings about us). When something as wonderful as you happens to a guy, he sure isn't going to let anything like school spoil his hopes. You have made me very proud Brent. To be able to know a girl like you well enough to love her was more than I expected and also to have her care for me! I'm very lucky and very happy.

You are very much what I want Brent, so much so I still can't believe you are real. My love for you is the strongest part of my being, but at the same time it is also hauntingly beautiful and delicate. It is what I rely on for strength, it houses my fondest hopes and memories. Love is a very confusing, yet wonderful thing for a guy like me.

'I have to hit the sack now. Study hard girl. Take care of yourself. God bless you Brent. I love you. Steve.

N

Wow! Brent was overcome with the intensity of this letter, so beautifully written to her from such an intense young man. Brent paused to savor the gift she had been given with this letter. The letter evoked the emotions Brent thought would surface upon reading, again, the first letters from Steve. Pleasant memories, grief, the thoughts of how much was lost, surged through her psyche, and then acceptance, again.

A "scab" grows over your wounded heart; but like most scabs, it gets picked away and leaves a scar. Over time, the scar lightens and is invisible to others; but, is a constant reminder to the wounded person, and often keeps them, over the years, from disclosing all they feel.

N

September 19, 1963: Dear Brent, Sorry about not writing sooner. Things have been sort of rocky. As they say in the service: "The situation is still fluid."

Thanks very much for writing to me every day. It helped to have you a little closer. You were a good sport to put up with the silence, but your letters mean so much to me. I would have tried to repay you in some small way, if I had been able. I wish I could say things to you that would mean as much to you as your letters have meant to me. Love, Steve.

September 22, 1963: Dear Brent, My mother talked quite a bit about your little talk with her. She told me to take real good care of such a precious? (The word I wanted wouldn't come; the only ones I could think of seemed somehow belittling, when compared to what you are.) She is very happy for us. She was very young also, when she met my father. We somehow remind her of days not so long ago. Love, Steve.

September 24, 1963: Dear Steve, Just remember Steve that I am very human; so don't put me on to much of a pedestal, even though I do love it up there. I sure don't want to disappoint you in any way. Remember dear that I think of you always, and may God take care of you. Did your mother ever tell you not to write anything in a letter that you wouldn't want put on the front page of the local newspaper? Mind did and you know, I think it is good advice. Don't you? With all my love Steve, Brent

September 24, 1963: Dear Brent. I'm serious when I say you can tell me these things. I will not think you are feeling sorry for yourself. I lean on you. Lean on me a little; I promise to nod in all the right places. I love and need you Brent. Things like this are not going to disappear because people are people and are by no means perfect. I'm working hard for our hopes. You really have done something to this Joe. I don't know, but it sounds like love. God bless you and our hopes Brent. I hope with all my heart they come true. I love you very much. Love, Steve.

N

Brent reflected on what she may have revealed to her future mother-in-law about her home life. Her father was a "spare the rod, spoil the child" type of disciplinarian. There has been, for sure, a much worse parent in the world than Brent's father; but, even with that thought, he did not always endear himself to them with some of his "religious" based beliefs. There were memories of him not allowing his son to play organized sports on Sundays; or at school, of having her made to sit alone in the classroom, while the other students participated in a dance activity. If your transgressions were bad enough, in his perception, they would earn you a few slaps with a leather belt. It is not that this happened that often, as we had been quick learners.

The last time he picked up the strap to "discipline" her came as a shock to her as she was older, although in those years she was not yet the legal age of twenty-one. And, she was dating Steve by then! She and her dad were discussing something, that is now lost to her memory; but she had contradicted his beliefs about the matter.

Much to her amazement he had reached for the strap and had stepped towards her; whereupon, she had grabbed onto it and defied him to hit her. His reply was: "Who is going to stop me?! "Good question," she had toyed with for a second; and then, the words she had heard herself say were: "Steve Martin will!!" Her father composed himself immediately, put the strap away, and never threatened her with it again. Steve Martin had obviously reached a high level of respect in her father's eyes, and she was his problem now! And, Steve Martin was to be her hero forever.

On the other hand, Brent would have assured her future mother-in-law that her mother was the voice of reason in the home and that her brother was her best friend and confidant growing up. Ironically, her brother was the initiator of her visit to the college campus where she had met Steve, at a "DANCE!" Her brother was there from the very beginning of Steve being in her life, and he was to be there at the end.

September 30, 1963: Dear Brent. What do you think about partridge hunting? It could be a chance to get out and do a little walking. After a week bending over books, it would do you good. It would also give you a chance to see what all the Martin men (and boys) do during the Fall. Might be of some use in the near future. Love, Steve

N

This could have been Brent's "Waterloo!" They did go "hunting." He carried his gun, and Brent trudged along behind him. That was the problem. She trudged along! After the "hunt," he very patiently explained to her the proper way to walk through the forest; without giving an alarm to all the "hunted" in the area. Actually, Brent doesn't recall any pressure to join him hunting again!

N

September 30, 1963: Dear Steve, A funny thing happened walking back from supper last night. Two other girls and myself were, as usual, talking a mile a minute. Suddenly one of them looks at me and says, "Do you love him?" Now if that isn't a direct question! So not to be outdone by her directness, I told her in a serious tone of voice that: "I love him very much." She seemed quite taken by the idea. She said she has never seen anyone like that.

I guess I am quite lucky. Can you image anyone asking me what it is like to be in love? I can remember asking that question not so very long ago myself. It is true that time takes care of a lot of things. My worst problem is trying to hasten time, but I think I'm learning.

I have been reading your letters over again. I love every one of them, and I miss you very much tonight. I hope you are in good spirits. It's dreadful when I start missing you like this. I like to just sit and think about the way you look and the things you say. It is so wonderful to have someone as great as you to love. I see everything good for us in the future. You are the only person in the world that makes me feel as though there is no other more desirable place in the world to be, than when I'm with you.

All my ambitions seem to be directed to you now. There will be no greater place on earth than wherever our home is. It is going to be so filled with love. Until that time, I intend to fill every letter and every hour that we are together with love. I love you very much, Brent.

October 1, 1963: Dear Brent, You know Joe, (A new nickname?) I don't recognize this guy writing to you. He is very different from the guy I used to know. I like this guy a lot better. He is working for something, not wandering anymore.

Look Brent, that kid is wearing that grin again. Believe me, it says all the things he can't find word to express. Love, Steve.

October 3, 1963: Dear Brent, My every thought concerns us Brent. I keep catching myself just staring off into space simply thinking about the way things are going to be. They are going to be very wonderful for me, Brent. I pray they will mean as much to you. You deserve nothing but happiness, Brent. My happiness will come only if you are very happy. I want so very much for us, Brent. With hard work we will be able to claim that happiness. We have got such a head start on that happiness. A down payment on a star.

I feel so very close to you Brent. All week you have been here by my side. (Keeping me from throwing things.) I'm coming home Brent. I'm coming home. I just want to see you. If you see that grin, you had better run. Love you Brent. God bless you Brent.

October 7, 1963: Dear Steve, The girls are really something here. Instead of saying: Hi, how are you?" They say: "Hi, did you see him?"

We both seem to live our memories and our dreams through writing. But someday "our" dreams will come true. You mean everything wonderful and good in this world to me. I hope you realize this, for my world would be very hopeless now without you. You are such an integral part of me now that any hardship to you hurts me also. Take care now and come home safely. Love, Brent.

October 9, 1963: Dear Brent, Actually Brent, we are very lucky. Suppose we had nothing but memories and no dreams, or only dreams. No matter how you look at it we could only be worse off than we are. As for myself, I feel I'm the luckiest guy in the world. I would not change one dream or memory. I realize now Brent, that this is the way you feel when you have found the one you were meant for. I hope you share this.

Love was meant to be shared. Not only have we shared this, but also our dreams, the things we stand for, and our everyday problems. To me this is a strong foundation to build a lasting relationship upon. How I could have lived the years before I met and cared for you, I don't know. Now it seems impossible, you are so much a part of me.

Everything good and beautiful I see in the world around me, reminds me of you and my love for you. You are the type of girl Brent, I'm always proud to be seen with. Nothing gives me greater pleasure than to introduce you to my friends and members of the Martin tribe. You never fail to impress people. It does my ego a world of good.

I feel very close to you Brent. Each and every day I think of you and wish you were near, a thousand times over. I love you very much Brent.

Why I was blessed I don't know. I only thank God that I was so lucky. God bless you Brent. Love, Steve.

October 10, 1963: Dear Brent, When you can visit my campus, I intend to walk you around the path we followed the first time I met you. I may be a sentimental fool, but I'm not trying to recapture anything. I have so much more now. All I am doing is going back for a moment, to a time in my life when suddenly everything changed. It is the place and time I started to fall in love with a very special girl. A girl, it seemed, had been meant just for me. Now that summer has passed, I want to return and follow that path with my girl, that special girl.

(The visit to Steve's campus did occur several months later and was mentioned in a letter from one of his friends several years later. They did not walk the path again as they didn't want to ignore their guests that night.)

October 13, 1963: Dear Steve, I feel so very thankful tonight for having you Steve. You mean so very much to me. Being able to talk to you and to communicate my feelings to someone like you is the most wonderful thing in the world. I disliked coming back to school and leaving you. I felt like crying for missing you so. I guess I let it show too much. My friends are getting wise.

All my goals are directed to you and for us to be together. There is nothing in the future for me unless you want me for always Steve. I feel very certain that you do, and it makes me very happy. I only hope that you will always be proud of me. What you think is everything in the world to me. I love you with all my heart, mind, and soul. I am sure our life together will be one of the most wonderful examples of love and happiness ever. So, good night sweet prince and sweet dreams. I love you. Brent

October 23, 1963, Dearest Brent. I can't ever hope to tell you what you mean to me now. I have the most important thing in the world. I have a girl (the most wonderful girl I have ever known) who truly loves me. We share a feeling that is really nameless and ageless, yet basic to all mankind. A feeling that is a way to live your life. It is something too few people ever find, say nothing about share. I no longer think of myself alone. You are always there; it is just the natural way for things to be. When I say something, I feel I'm speaking for you too. I hope you feel this. It is wonderful. There is no longer a completely separate me. You have become a very important part of me. It is very nice being so much in love. No fears. Just the knowledge that the future holds so very much for us. We will be very happy.

No two people will have shared so much, so completely. While I don't believe that I'm anything very special (except that I have you) I firmly believe that you and I share something very special. Our love is special. Our life together will be special. See Joe, I'm a maniac, but don't tell Brent! I would hate losing her. I would be losing part of myself.

I love you very much Brent. I miss you. I'm very happy and very proud. I'm the luckiest guy in the world! I pray you will always be very happy. You deserve so very much more than "better than average." You deserve everything beautiful and perfect to your wishes. I hope you never get the feeling that things could have gone better. (Note: Little did we know the worst would happen.) I love you. Study hard, take care, and have fun. God bless you Brent. Love, Steve.

October 27, 1963: Dearest Steve, Happy sixth month anniversary to you and me. We are sure to see many more of them, I'm sure.

Before I forget to tell you; if someday this week you don't get a letter from me, it will be due to our freshman initiation. The grapevine says it is really time consuming. So don't worry if a letter doesn't arrive. I'm thinking of you always. I will make every effort to write. I need to tell you everything that goes on. It should be fun, but one can never tell.

I am very proud of you Steve for the decisions you have made. I know I wasn't much help Saturday night, but I realized what you meant. It is just that I love you so desperately, and I want to spend every possible minute with you.

When I am in your arms there is nothing in the world that can touch me or bother me. I feel completely safe and at home. I'm living for the day that we will be together for always. We have had six months of knowing each other. It is such a short time actually, but it was when my life truly began. Right now Steve, the time when we can be together forever seems to be so far away. It seems at times, like right now, I can't stand to wait. For some reason Steve, I feel very confused and mixed up tonight. I don't know what's gotten into me all of a sudden. I'm just the type that always sees the grass is greener on the other side, I guess. I am just a glutton for punishment.

Just a while ago when you first met me, I was a little girl who was going to be a registered nurse and who thought the idea of marriage for someone so young was quite unthinkable. Now here I am wishing that I could jump into it this very minute. When I think of my age it still scares me, but in my heart it seems to be all I want. I want to face the world with you Steve. I want to help you make a place for "us" in this world. I want you to have the best possible chance to achieve. But, oh I wish I could be there with you. I want to be a wife to you Steve. I want to try to make you as happy as your mother has made your dad. I wonder how I can best go about doing this.

Right now I feel like saying to heck with all of this for me. I feel more like combining efforts and just getting you through school.

Now I suppose I need a good talking to! But now I feel better for having admitted what I was thinking. Oh Steve, I'm in an awful mood. Well, now I know why your mother used to cry after your father would call her when he was in the Army. You haven't called me tonight, but for some reason the faucet is sure turned on. I'm sorry Steve. Well, at least you can say a girl cried over you, once upon a time. I love you very deeply Steve. Good night for now. God bless you. Love always, Your Brent.

October 27, 1963: Dearest Brent. Boy, I have started really missing you already. But you know "Joe" I would not have it any other way. "Joe," I love that Brent so very much. I don't know which way is up and I don't care.

Please take care of yourself Brent. I don't know what I would do without you. If something happened to you, a very large part of me would be missing also. No "one more try." I have found the girl of my dreams. No one or nothing will ever measure up to her. I never believed that a person like you actually existed. You are the girl every guy dreams about. The girl he measures all others beside. The one he never quite finds. But I found her, last night she was in my arms. I wish she was right now.

I am very lucky. I love Brent, she loves me. My parents like her very much. Why even my dog "Tiger" knows that the girl Steve sees is a wonderful, lovely girl. (With a human mother like that, who needs a canine girlfriend.)

I love you so much. There is no price on the feelings that pass between us. No value can be put on our relationship. No one but God actually knows how much we mean to each other. Our relationship has gone beyond the scope of what mere mortal minds can fathom. We can only see, feel, love, and believe it. I can ask no more of life than you and this. I love you. I miss you. God bless you Brent. Love, Steve.

October 29, 1963: Dearest Steve, Our freshman initiation is in full swing this week! We are not supposed to eat between meals, but I'm being bad. I'm eating the cookies my mother made for me. So there, you "lowly and humble juniors!" This is what we have to say to them: "I, most low and humble "pro-be" (probationer) do bow down to show my respect to you most high and honorable junior (or instructor)."

It is almost 4:30 p.m. and I'm still waiting to get permission to get my mail. Isn't it awful? It's a letter from you too, and I want to read it! You know Steve, you are a wonderful "Joe." When I'm doing these dumb things, I think about you and think: If only you could see me now!" You would laugh your head off.

I love you very much Steve. You are a strong support for me, and you are now the most important thing in my life. I too have no need to look any further. There is no one else who could measure up to you in any way. There would always be something missing. You know I had an image too. It probably wasn't quite as well developed as your image of the ideal person for you; but it was there with many strong points, as you soon found out!

It took me a little longer to trust completely than it did you. I have seen too many trusts broken. Maybe that is why I was the way I was. But I do trust you completely Steve. I've always wanted a trust like ours, and it is a rather novel and wonderful thing when you do honestly find it. I love you very much Steve. It is something subtle and undefinable. It is a feeling that we have between us. It is a feeling that life would never be the same or as bright without the other one. If I ever lost you Steve, I could never love or trust so deeply ever again. I know there will be difficult times. There always is for everyone, but I know that together we will overcome them.

My prime objective now is to be with you. I feel that is the most important thing. I no longer feel like a separate being. I'm working along beside you for a special goal there on the horizon. You are a wonderful man Steve. I could not ask for any better. I don't know how I was so lucky, so soon. It is a wonderful thing I believe, and I cherish it very much. I love you Steve with all my being. Good night for now. I think of you always. Love forever, Brent.

P.S. Your letters should go down in the books of "The Greatest Love Letters Of The World." They are beautiful, Steve. I mean it. They say so very much. All my love, Brent

(Years later while re-reading these letters; Brent stopped to recall that when they started writing the letters in the spring of 1963, Steve was only 19 years old, and she was only 18 years old.)

November 3, 1963: Dearest Steve, Wow, did I just barely make it! I got back to the dorm tonight at 6:05! Fortunately, the girl who signed me out Friday, happened to be at the door. She opened it for me! I rushed into the office, signed in, and raced up the stairs and down the hall to my room. I saw a friend on the way, and thank heavens I didn't stop to talk.

I left my coat and everything in my room and went up the hall to the bathroom. Just about then the House Mother walked in the door, asking for another girl. Another friend was there and told her maybe the girl she was looking for was in the library. Actually, our mutual friend was hiding in the closet of the girl who suggested the library! I was so thankful she wasn't looking for me. If that wasn't luck! I don't think I'll cut it that close again.

I wish I could stay with you. I think every Sunday night when I come back here that I will just sit down and cry. It sort of helps. Also, I must talk with Bonnie because she is going through the same thing.

Thank you so much for the Promise PIN darling! I am so happy to have such a meaningful symbol of showing the world our commitment to each other for a future life together. My brother is very pleased, and my mother is too. My friends here have given their congratulations also.

I'm so very proud Steve! I love you so very much. I know that I can't do anything different from what I am doing right now; but, it's still so hard to be away from you. I know I must take things in order, but it is so hard to wait. I never knew that love could so completely drive one nuts! It helps so much to have you talk to me. It is good to have one level head in this partnership.

Let me see. I must think of this week as one long work day, at the end of which I shall see you. I can do the laundry (Nursing class). Write out our meal plan (Nutrition class). Do a little cooking (Chemistry class). Decide why the "baby" is crying (Psychology class). Prepare the fried chicken for dinner (Anatomy & Physiology class). Then adjust to my present situation (Professional Adjustment class)! How is that for imagination? You know, it just might work.

I must get to sleep now and get up early to study. I mean plan "our meals" (Nutrition exam)! Good night for now. I love you Steve. Love forever, Brent.

N

The Birthday Cake: The weekend Brent had just returned to school from had included the celebration of Steve's 20th birthday. Brent had baked a birthday cake for him. Being relatively new to the family, still a little shy, and not wanting to disrupt the event with giving him the cake right after the meal, as she knew his mother had a cake for him also; she suggested a walk outside.

It was a chilly November evening, and a soft snow was quietly falling around them as she retrieved the cake from the car and lit the candles. Light emanated from windows in the house, snow started swirling around them. In the glow of the lighted candles Brent presented Steve with the cake. She was immediately rewarded with his pleasure, probably not so much that it was a great cake, but that she had made it for him.

Brent always remembered that first birthday celebration with him and the closeness they felt that evening.

N

November 5, 1963: Dearest Brent. You know Brent, something just dawned on me. We are wonderfully suited for each other. I love you and you love me. I want you for my wife and mother of my children. You want me as your husband and the father of your children. We believe in one another. We completely trust each other. When one of us gets overly "home" sick for the other, the other remains level headed. It is really something to share such a relationship. I don't have to work on this as it comes very naturally to me.

Wondering what brought all this on? Well, I was returning from the book store. It was a nice quiet night, sort of on the cold side. I was thinking of you and us, per usual. I keep thinking how much I love and miss you Brent. Oh, if you only knew how much I love and miss you. It was here that I realized, because you feel the same; maybe you were thinking the same thing at the exact same time. For the rest of it, it was easy from there on in.

You know my parents are really very proud of you. My father was just as bad as my mother about your cake. He never misses a chance to make a good point about Brent. Why, you are not even "my girl" anymore. The rest of my family has taken you right into the family. Yes darling, they are very proud of you and of my choice. I am too. God bless you Brent. Love, Steve.

November 19, 1963: Dear Steve, You know Steve, my dad thinks you are a very nice guy. Chalk one up for you! My mother also thinks you are nice and she is happy for me also.

(The letter continued with plans for the Thanksgiving Holiday. Also, letters from Brent were beginning to express her doubts about staying in nursing school.)

N

November 22, 1963: Brent and her classmates were looking forward to the long Thanksgiving weekend. Suddenly the news of the assassination of President John F. Kennedy shocked the nation. The mood became subdued as the girls were being picked up by their families.

Much to Brent's surprise, Steve was with her dad when he arrived to pick her up. Steve had hiked from college and her dad had picked him up on the way. Steve had not heard the news and thought maybe her dad had been mistaken! Brent assured him that her dad was correct and that the President had, indeed, been shot and had died.

N

December 1, 1963: Dear Brent, I wish that once in a while I could be with you and not feel when I leave you, that I have not seen you long enough. When I am with you Brent, the time passes so fast. I guess I'll have to marry you to solve that problem. You know Brent, I love you very much. When I got back to campus today I was so tied up inside I could not talk, even to Rich. You mean everything to me. You are my entire world. I need you very much. Every time I see you, I love and want you more and more. At one time I thought I loved you completely. But as time goes on I find I love you more and more. You are finding parts of me I never knew existed. You are demanding and getting love from me I never knew I had inside. You have not got a chance! I am going to marry you, and I am going to make you very happy. See, just "talking" to you, and I feel alright. But I mean every word. See you soon "Mrs." Love, Steve.

December 8, 1963: To my darling Steve. Do you know I love you very much, that I'm very proud of you, that you are all my dreams come true, my life, my hope, my entire world. I miss you so very much that it hurts.

My mother says if we both want each other, we will be sure to make it happen! Isn't that wonderful! I think she is pulling for us. Everyone likes my Steve. How can they help it! I can't! When he flashes that dazzling smile, I haven't got a chance.

I love the pin you gave me, and what it stands for as the promise of our future together.

I love you with all the love I have. I want to be with you so very much. I miss you dreadfully.

Good night for now darling. I'll see you in my dreams. Love, Brent.

A

CHANGE

OF

PLANS!

(NURSING? FORESTRY?)

Chapter 4

A Change Of Plans

January 8, 1964: Dearest Steve, Well, today was "D-Day." I have theoretically gotten through one of the most difficult steps of my nurses training. Around 10:00 a.m. today we were suddenly called to go view a post-mortem. I was sort of shaken up before I went in, but once in there, it wasn't very bad. No one in our group fainted! The doctor was very good. He asked us questions and it was instructive. We also had our beloved Dr. Eckels there, a father figure, so that was nice. It was really worse for one of the girls as the patient had been one of hers the day before.

In retrospect, it was sort of funny the reaction we had. We had been spoken to about "posts" yesterday to prepare us, but we didn't know when they would have one. At 8:00 a.m. we had our anatomy class. After class we had two hours before chemistry class. Suddenly one of the girls was out in the hall calling us. We went out and she informed us that we had to go see a post-mortem!

My old nerves hit high gear about then. I wanted to go and get it done, so I grabbed my apron (which I had taken off) and my coat. Over half the class was available to go. While standing outside the door of the Necropsy Room I looked down, and my apron was going back and forth—my knees were shaking!

It was quite an experience. Everyone thought it was interesting. Well, that is enough of that. Good night. Love, Brent.

January 16, 1964: Dearest Brent, You make me feel as if I were the luckiest guy in the world Brent. When I think of all the love, under-standing, and trust you have so selflessly given me; I know that I am the luckiest guy alive. I am very happy also, Brent. I never thought that there was a person like you in this world, Brent. And then one day, there you were. I never knew any one person could be so very sincere and yet be very beautiful and desirable. A combination of physical and moral beauty found far too seldom. And yes, I was lucky enough to find you.

I am sure that our love is something that is planned to be lasting. A living thing to grow and flower with the years. We were destined to spend our lives together. We share so very much now. And darling, it will only get better and better.

I am afraid darling that you are stuck with a guy who plans to court his favorite girl the rest of his life. She will always be his girl in his eyes, no matter how many years have passed. His love and devotion will grow like the young, living thing it is. It will have the blessing of eternal youth, even while the two lovers themselves grow old.

I am glad I brought those pictures with me. I get one of those grins every time I look at them. I like the one of you and my mother. You both look very happy. Two generations of wives for Martin men are represented in that one photo. One day we will have fun sitting in front of a fireplace, during a roaring snow storm, and looking at these and other pictures.

You have made my life so very much more meaningful Brent. I am very proud of you. I only hope I can give you everything you so richly deserve. You have given me so much love, understanding, and trust darling. I hope I return some of these very great and wonderful gifts. I have received the most revered gift any woman can give, her true and undying love. I can't say any more than—"I love you."

I will always believe this is my greatest reward in life. It is very much more than I ever thought I would ever ask of life.

Good night darling. May good times walk with you. I love you very much. I will see you soon. We are one day closer. And soon darling, we will be one night to "home." Good night, Steve.

January 22, 1964: Dearest Steve. It seems I am running out of paper. What does one do in that event? Perhaps I should get some more. You see how brilliant I am. I actually figured that one out. That was probably more than I did on the chemistry exam!

The time has come when I have to work the wards on the weekends. I won't be getting home but every other weekend. This really cramps our style!

Last night, about 9:00 o'clock, I went over to the Out Patient Department because I have something which looks like a rash. Everyone thought I had measles or chicken pox. This is the second time for me to be sick here. If it is around, I catch it. I think this is how I manage to get sympathy! This morning I saw another doctor, and she said it is only a fungus!?

Say Steve, I just thought of something again for "our" Honeymoon. I think I would like to go to Pennsylvania, to the Dutch farming area. I have heard it is beautiful country. You see, I keep coming up with ideas. They will probably change a hundred times. It is fun to dream anyway!

Now we have had a water fight with our syringes. It was fun though. Without the needle they make wonderful water pistols! Good night for now darling. I love you very much. Love, forever, Brent.

January 27, 1964: Dearest Brent, It seems very funny to be home and writing to you. I guess before we are done we will have written the other from may an odd place.

The sunset tonight darling, made me think very much of you and "us." We are very much like a beautiful sunset. We are seeing the sun set on our childhood; and out of the dark of adolescence, is appearing a man and a woman. Tomorrow we will see the sun rise upon our life together, as well as our adulthood.

For darling, somewhere in the darkness, I found you. And soon Brent, we will see the sunrise together, side by side, the way we are meant to be. I am very glad I found you so soon. With you beside me Brent, things now have a "why." The future belongs to us. Study hard darling. Love, Steve.

January 29, 1964: Dearest Steve, Hey there, you with the wonderful blue eyes, I love you. You are wonderful, sensitive, sensible, adorable, masculine, desirable, intelligent; and all mine!

It was so nice to get a letter from you today. You say things in such a very nice way. I am beyond glad I found you so soon, too. It is so wonderful to know that you are there beside me all the time. I love you for your sensitivity to the world around you. You are able to make things seem so beautiful. You value the more holy and lasting things on earth and of life. You look at things and find deep meaning in them. You can look at the fields and mountains and see more than just rocks and dirt. You see I happen to love you very much! Brent.

February 3, 1964: Dearest Steve, Just to let you know, I have passed my exams! It is nice to have them over. However, it is rather dizzying to see what we have ahead of us for the next semester. It includes: pharmacology, medical-surgical nursing, microbiology, sociology, diet therapy and nursing fundamentals-2. This, plus our ward duty. I have a headache right now just thinking about it all. Good night for now darling. I love you. Brent.

February 5, 1964: Dearest Kitten. Boy, I guess I learned which one of this family is working the hardest. I am sure that I couldn't handle the amount of credits that you are. At the same time, I am sure you are very capable to do just that. That's my Brent. I am very proud to have a girl such as her for my girl.

That is quite a schedule you have ahead of you. I didn't realize you began a new set of courses the same time we do. Remember, we are both working towards the same goal. Both of our jobs in this family are of the same importance. Goodnight Kitten, Steve.

February 19, 1964: Dearest Brent. We Forestry and Wildlife majors are looking forward to summer camp. Phil and I are planning quite a time for this summer. Can you see two guys like us turned loose in all that wilderness. I guess I will see a lot of sunsets alone this coming summer. I am really telling myself that this separation for you and me is very necessary. Phil and I have finally admitted to each other that we do love our girls, and that when we are finally able, we want to marry them. Phil has known for a long time that my feelings ran this way; but, he could not get me to admit it. He gave up first. He had me completely fooled. We kept telling each other that guys like us had no need to get married. Hunting and fishing meant too much to us. Actually, it is all pretty funny. We have to feed our male egos, you know. Good night Kitten. I love you, Steve.

February 20, 1964: Dearest Brent. To continue our discussion about marriage: I know we will not have half the problems some people have. Married life requires two mature people who both bring something into the relationship, as well as love. I have to keep telling myself this Brent. It is the only thing that keeps me here at college. That and the fact that I am a little stubborn. Even that would not have kept me here. The fact that I am working for our combined future has.

I love you very much Kitten. I miss you. I wish I was with you. I would welcome the warmth and love in your smile and arms. It would be nice to forget everything but you Kitten. There are so many things I want to talk about. Remember, smile that smile when I call you "Kitten." Then you are really all mine. Good night Kitten. Steve.

February 25, 1964: Dear Steve, I guess I lived on love Sunday night to Monday noon, as I didn't eat either supper or breakfast. Nothing appealed to me.

I know 'that' feeling too Steve, of wanting to prolong our leaving each other. Yet every time we leave, we are closer to returning to each other for good. Oh Steve, I love you so very much. I feel so happy right now. I feel so wonderful when I can visualize our life together. I have to remember that we are having a part of the life right now. We are separated by miles only.

By the way, our class picture will be in the paper this Sunday! Our class is the first class since 1951 to all be here in March. Also, two other things have happened. Liz, a patient, one of our instructors, and I will be in the newspaper as publicity for the nursing program. We also have been told our tuition will go up next year. Love, Your Kitten.

February 25, 1964: Dearest Brent, Reading your letters Kitten reminds me of how I feel when I get back after a weekend home. We are very much alike. I am also looking forward to the day you come home to me to stay. All our separations and all the rushing here and there is going to give way to a very wonderful marriage. I wish I was talking to you instead of your picture. Goodnight Kitten, Steve.

February 29, 1964: Dearest Brent, Brent you are going to be my bride. Never doubt this nor my desire for you to become my wife. Kitten, you and our dreams form the basis for my life. Without you there would be nothing but darkness. A darkness that not only surrounds you, but is a part of you. I need you and your love very much. This is something I would not tell anyone else but you. It is something only a husband can tell his wife freely. I tell you this freely and in all honesty. I want you beside me. I want to give you my love, and I want to receive yours. I want to give you strength, and I need yours. I need you Kitten, but I also have to give to you. You know Kitten, I feel we do all this! I love you Brent. I miss and need you ever so much. This isn't a little boy crying out in the darkness. It is a guy, who is becoming a man, telling the girl he loves of the feeling inside him and that makes him want to forget everything but her, and their young, beautiful love. Take care Kitten. You are not one of my possessions Brent; but you are the most precious thing in my life. Good night Kitten, Steve.

March 3, 1964: Dear Steve, Well darling, I hope you will be free April 5th! We are to be capped on that lovely day. We will look like real nurses then with our caps on. You know, I love the month of April. More wonderful things have happened to me in April, such as meeting you! The time separating us will be more bearable when I am through school. If I was out working and also saving for us; then, I think it might be slightly easier. I sure hope the military service doesn't interfere that much though. Time will tell. Our relationship gives me a lot of strength to keep going. There is no such feeling of warmth and security than when I am in your arms.

I am not quite sure about the obstacles I spoke about before. The biggest obstacles are those which time will remove. We have some control over them, but we are doing what we have to do now. We can't get around school. That would be a foolish thing to do, especially where we are on the winning side. However, we must keep in mind the fact that we can't wait until things are absolutely perfect to get married; because that time will never come. We will always be in a state of imbalance as far as material things are concerned. As soon as school is over we will be the most ready to get married as any other time in our life. We will have reached a level of maturity then, which will be only bettered by our being together and working together.

So darling, as soon as we finish this school obstacle, we will be able to face the world on an equal basis. We will have the tools to fight with. With our combined efforts we will really come out on top. I have great faith in us Steve.

I love you darling. You are the world to me. We have a wonderful life, and I think about you all the time. You are my wonderful dream come true. With all my love forever. Brent.

P.S. Have to tell you! I came out on top on my pharmacology test. The funny part is what my instructor wrote on it: You have done very, very well. This was a difficult test. She also said she took the test herself and that I got a better grade than she did! At least I don't feel like such a doodoo now, and maybe there is hope for me yet. Love, Brent.

March 5, 1964: Dearest Brent, I hope that we are able to reach our little star before three years pass. As soon as you are out of school; and I have a good job, you can expect me to ask you to come home as soon as you can.

I don't know how the service will enter into this, but before I ask you, I am going to know exactly what is going on. If chances are that I will get drafted, I will enlist! No matter what happens Kitten, you are going to get asked, and you will have to say either "yes!" or "maybe." I will not take "no!" for your answer. So when the time comes, remember this.

Always remember this "Joe" loves you Kitten. Your home with him will always be waiting for you. You see Kitten, he has no home until you can come to him. It is nice when things work both ways. Goodnight Kitten, Steve.

March 20, 1964: Dearest Kitten, Today was really the first day of spring. Our zoology lab class went to York Beach, and it was a very lovely day. There was almost no wind and you could see for miles. The Isle of Shoals was clearly visible, as well as those picturesque lobster boats that trade in and about York Harbor. It was really quite a day.

We managed to see a large number of various sea fowl and birds over the course of the entire afternoon. It almost seemed they too, were welcoming the arrival of spring. A large number of these were species I had never seen before. We were really very lucky. With no tourist at York yet, there was nothing but one's self, the ocean, and miles of coast line. There is something about the sea that make a person look deep inside himself.

Yesterday afternoon at the beach, I finally realized why I want my degree so very much. It leads me to an accomplished end. There is something fascinating about the raw power of nature. She exists in a manner that all of us could pattern our lives after. She is very powerful, yet she is also very complicated. She moves always towards some end; yet the method she employs is governed by only God. There is an order in her that can leave no doubt in one's mind that there must be some higher being.

Talking about the idea that nature is an example to pattern our lives after, Rich and I got off on a new topic. Is a man an animal, or isn't he? Rich cannot quite believe that he is an animal. Is not an animal a being that follows solely its instincts? If so, where does that leave man? By one argument it leaves him an animal. By another it leaves him something more. I have not decided for myself, but I seem to be settling somewhere in the middle. I suppose someone has already answered that one, but it is fun to discuss.

All kidding aside, Rich and I have really had some great talks. Most of them break up late in the night. We must learn to "hunt" with our minds. Not only hunt, but at times find answers. You and I have had some really good talks also; have we not Brent?

You know Kitten, we have life right by the tail. Let us really shake the dust out of the old girl. There are a lot of dawns and sunsets in our lives Kitten, and no two are alike. Let us see all of them that we can. Our life together is too much to simply think about.

It has to be lived day by day, minute by minute. You and I will get the most possible out of our life. Without you Kitten, this would not be possible for me. You are my world Brent. Good night Kitten, Steve.

March 25, 1964: Dearest Steve, I just got through re-reading the first 21 letters you have written to me. They are very wonderful and bring back memories. Darling, I'm glad you see me the way you do. I only want to be your girl. I'm glad if you are proud of me. Yet the most wonderful part is being the one you know as the girl who loves you. I do love you so very much, and I am so proud of you too. I love to know the man I want for my husband is very capable and yet very warm and understanding. See you at the Capping ceremony! Love, Brent.

April 5, 1964: Dearest Steve, So now the Capping ceremony is past. Seeing you dearest, was wonderful. However nice it was to finally get my nurses cap, I counted it as very little as compared to my joy of having you there. I would have forfeited everyone else there for me just to have you with me. No kidding Darling, I could have torn that little white cap to shreds if it would have made it possible for me to go with you. I really hated school for keeping us apart. I wonder almost to what avail it is. They make everything look so blame glamorous and everything. They don't tell how hard it is to be separated from the one you love the most in this crazy old world.

I know for sure now that the happiest day of my life will be the day we are married and go off together to face the world. I miss you desperately darling. I can see you very vividly Steve. I can feel the warmth of your wonderful lips on mine and the strength in your arms around me. I love you very dearly. I can see your smile and hear you laugh. Darling, please have that wonderful look on your face!

You know I have never known such happiness as you give me. Darling, I want to come home so very much. Why do we have to be so level headed? It is so awful at times. Just anyone try to separate us after we are married. Darling, please ask me to come home as soon as you can. I want my home with my husband very much.

So back to work again. Thank you for a wonderful time Darling. No one will keep us apart soon. When we are together we do have a wonderful time, don't we! Good night for now my dearest Steve. Love, Brent.

April 5, 1964: Dearest Brent, I am very proud of you Kitten. Seeing you capped meant an awful lot to me. I am very glad you wanted me to be there. We have made it this far, the rest is all downhill. I am the luckiest guy in the world.

I am sorry I could not see you any more than I did this last vacation. To be honest "our" time has not really arrived yet, but it will. We are going through school to help our parents as well as ourselves. Once we are out, we really start on our own.

I am very glad I found you so very early Kitten. I would not change a single precious moment. You have made some of the very rough moments of growing up very smooth. I hope I give you as much darling.

The goal of our marriage and having you always close to me has given me a reason to want the future and what it holds. That we are not able to give each other now all the love each of us feels, makes the future a very bright and warm place. There, free from external forces, simply as a man and a woman, we can find the eternal fulfillment of our love.

There are times Kitten, I would give anything to throw off the bonds of society and those of the older, wiser lovers to welcome with open arms the wonderful woman I am to marry. But, we must do everything in perfect order. The requirements of our own society and those of parental love must be satisfied, that is, if their requirements are within reason. We will feel a lot better for it.

Once again Brent, thank you for asking me to be present at your Capping. I am very proud of you Kitten. And, thank you for loving this "Joe." He loves you very much. He feels quite lost tonight. I hope that you are very happy about us Brent. I am. Goodnight Kitten, Steve.

April 7, 1964: Dearest Kitten, Your letter of the fifth was wonderful Kitten. Everything about our relationship makes me very happy and so very sure of a wonderful future.

Just think Brent, we are nearly through our first year. At the end of two more years our lives will finally be really our own. You may expect me to be hanging around quite a bit after that. And, as soon as I wear your resistance down, you can also expect to have me ask you to marry me.

I really do not know what I should think about our present relationship. How can just talking to a person mean so very much? How are we able to give and receive so much love and understanding while we are, on the surface just going together. I guess what really counts is how we feel deep inside of ourselves. There is no age limit on the ability to love.

I thought you might like to read the following, Kitten. It somehow manages to say some of the things my tongue has proved to be too dull to say. I can only tell you my heart is not so quiet, to me it sings a very beautiful melody. A melody I would never heard, if Kitten had not entered my life. Thank Kitten for me, will you Brent! Good night Kitten.

SONNET CXVI (16)
By William Shakespeare

Let me not to the marriage of true minds
Admit impediments. Love is not love
Which alters when it alteration finds,

Or bends with the remover to remove:
Oh, no! it is an ever-fixed mark,
That looks on tempests and is never shaken;
It is the star to every wandering bark,
Whose worth's unknown, although his height be taken.
Love's not Time's fool, though rosy lips and cheeks
Within his bending sickle's compass come;
Love alters not with his brief hours and weeks,
But bears it out even to the edge of doom.
If this be error and upon me proved,
I never writ, nor no man ever loved.

April 9, 1964: Dearest Steve. I love you Steve. I enjoyed your last letter very much. But, I think we are a little more than just "going together!" The poem was very nice. William Shakespeare. Wow! You know our letters are almost a good diary. When I read your last letters they reminded me of what we have done already. I am looking forward to seeing you again. By the way, that is what I live for. I'm glad I have the privilege of being your girl. Good night for now darling. Love, Brent.

April 9, 1964: Dearest Brent. Again, I am so very glad that Capping went so well for you Brent. I am only sorry I could not have shared more of it with you. No matter what Kitten, my thoughts and love are always very close to you. It makes no difference where my physical being is, part of my spiritual being is always there close by the one it loves most in this world. My hand will always be there on your right shoulder Kitten, just as you hand is on my shoulder. No Kitten, I am never really very far from you. Love, understanding, and trust are not affected by miles nor time.

When you give someone these wonderful gifts they remain always with that person. The love within me is yours Kitten; the love within you is mine. This is why I am always close to part of you Kitten, and you also a part of me. Because our love is part of each of us. Miles mean nothing to it because it does not come by mail, or it is not thrown, but because it is part of our very being. Good night Kitten, Steve.

April 20, 1964: Dearest Brent, A very good evening to you Kitten. I hope you are wearing that very special smile. I feel very happy tonight, in fact, I got on a cloud last Saturday night, and I have not got off yet. You know something else, I plan to take up permanent residence up here. Will you join me Kitten? I want you here beside me very much. Without my Kitten there could be no cloud up here for me.

I love you Kitten. You run down the hall, or where ever they may be, and tell those girls you were with last Friday night, that they can bet their lives that we are going to be married. Actually, I only really care about what you think, Kitten.

We shall have to go off somewhere by ourselves and just talk. It would seem so very pleasant not to have to worry about getting here or there in a short while. I am going to tell you about all my dreams, Brent. The things I want for "us." Just to put my head in your lap and tell you all about the dreams I have had inside me for so long. I never thought any of them would really come true. But now the biggest dream will be true. It is greater and much more wonderful than I ever dared hope. You are such a warm and soft person Kitten, yet you are also a very capable person.

In a very little while Kitten you will be my wife. The future looks very bright to me, Brent. Together, you and I are going to be very happy. Right now we have a remarkable amount of understanding in our relationship and our mutual trust is growing day by day.

I love you Brent. I need you. Please need me. Think of me as your husband. I want to give to you Brent, as well as take. You give so very much. We have gone far beyond the "going steady" stage Kitten. You are my wife. I am not able to be with you; but, I can't think of you any differently! You are the most important person in my life. You and I can win a very wonderful place in life for us and our family. Good night Kitten, Steve.

April 27, 1964: Dearest Steve. Happy Anniversary Darling! Do you remember that exactly one year ago I was dancing with you? That was the luckiest day of my life. What a lot this year has meant, and it has been the happiest one of my life.

Every year spent with you will be better and better. I love you very deeply Steve. Our love is not to be taken lightly, and it means so very much to both of us. I hope you are as happy as I am tonight. I believe you are.

Darling, I wanted to ask you if you save all my letters or not? Just curiosity, I guess. Mr. Martin, I think you are just about as wonderful as anyone could ask for. I love you very much, Sir. It is so wonderful to plan for our life together. I'm very proud of you darling! I am thinking of you constantly. Love forever. Your kitten, Brent.

April 27, 1964: Dearest Brent, Happy Anniversary Kitten! A year ago today I met my future wife. That beautiful girl was fated to be the most precious thing in my life. I love you very much Kitten. I pray we celebrate the fourth anniversary of this day as man and wife. It was very wonderful being with you this weekend Kitten.

There is more beauty in our relationship Kitten, than I ever thought there was present in the whole world. We make our own world. There is nothing but us and our love there. I love you Brent. You are one hell of a woman. God night Kitten, Steve.

May 3, 1964: Dearest Steve, Hello darling. I had to write to you tonight. It so happened I had several small things to do before tomorrow's classes. I still have to look up my patient's drugs that I gave Friday, but they can wait until tomorrow.

Thank you darling for a wonderful day. I am exhausted, but very happy in a painful way. I feel that one of the hardest ways to leave you is when returning back to school. It seems so awful leaving you there knowing you too have to face the old grind again. I feel like a criminal driving off, leaving my whole world, my life, there.

Darling, I am sorry if I make you feel sorry or guilty about us at times. I don't intend to make you feel that way. I have tried to explain what I have meant before, and I thought you understood. I trust you completely. It is frustrating to me at a time like that when I want to share with you, but also know, in my mind, that we have to go. I would never be able to leave you if I didn't start building up some resistance in myself. Never doubt that I love, and want, and need you as much as you have told me you want and need me. I love you so very desperately Steve. You are my whole world, my complete life all wrapped up in one wonderful, masculine form. You're the ultimate desire I have Steve. With all our trust and understanding, I would never doubt your intentions.

I have a desperate feeling when I have to leave you. It seems as though we are going through a storm now, an emotional storm. One of these times we are going to break out to the sunniest most wonderful day God ever created. That day we will be truly together as man and wife. Then, no one but God himself can separate us.

Good night for now my love. I can't tell you enough how much I love and need you. I want every blessed little thing you have ever said darling—except the gas stove! I don't have to say much of anything because you seem to voice our same opinions. Furthermore, I'm going to live with you, and I want to know your plans. Then, when I hear them, I have to agree because it all sounds so wonderful. Darling, this is your plan of life for us. I want you to tell me, and if there is something I don't like, I will be sure to tell you. I want your life and my life to be one so very much. I have no doubt about it Steve.

Good night darling. I hope you understand what I have tried to tell you. I love you and hope this means as much to you when I say it, as it means to me when you say it. Love forever, your Brent.

May 4, 1964: Dear Brent, You may not remember me Brent, but I met you at a dance here at the University over a year ago. I would like to marry you Brent. Would you become my wife? I realize that this is very sudden, but will you please think about it seriously. I guess I am just a guy that makes up his mind very quickly. So do not let that bother you. But take warning! I want you for my wife, and lady, you do not have a prayer of being anything but my wife.

Actually, I do not believe being my wife will be so bad. Of course this idea arises partly because I am an egoist. I plan to be close to my wife, closer than any other person on earth. My wife and I are going to see countless sunrises and sunsets together. Her eyes are going to shine with happiness, and my grin is going to echo that self-same happiness. She and I are going to be able to talk to each other. Her love will be the most important thing in this world for me.

We are going to have a nice little home. A place where anyone who enters it can feel the love and happiness that has taken up permanent abode there. They are going to live here quietly, and here they will enjoy life and each other to the fullest.

But, do you know something Kitten? They enjoy even more than this. When they are together in their love, they go to their own beautiful world where nothing except their love and the combination of their souls exist.

One day two children will be created out of their love. I want these children very much Kitten. To be able to bring forth life out of our love, it shows that God made our love the beautiful thing that it is.

I love you with my entire being Kitten. I never told you before Kitten, but if I some how lost you, I would never marry again. I know I could never love anyone as much as I love you, and to marry when I know it would not approach what our marriage would have been, would be a sacrilege. I would live and go on with my everyday life, but love of a woman would not have any place in my life thereafter.

I miss you an awful lot Brent. I miss the sound of your voice and the smell of your hair. I love and honor you Kitten. You are the most important thing in my world. I hope you had a good time this last weekend. I know I will look back to those happy memories. Good night Kitten, Steve

P.S. I love you with all my heart and soul Kitten. Will you marry me? I promise to love and honor you as the most wonderful person I know, until the end of   time.

May 6, 1964: Dearest Steve, Mr. Steven W. Martin, I am going to be most proud to be your wife. Nothing in the world can stop us from having that.

Darling, don't count on losing me. I stick hard and fast. Yet darling, if something should happen to me before we are one; I would want you to live the rest of your life as completely as you could. Neither of us could ever find in anyone else what we have found in each other. It would never be the same. Yet, if there was another woman in this world who loved you half as much as I do, I would want her to take care of you for me.

I couldn't stand to think of you alone with no one around who truly cared for you. It is hard enough in this world without being alone. Some child deserves to have you for a father. You are too wonderful a man to miss bringing up a son and/or daughter in this world, who would carry the fine traits that you have. Darling, I so want to be the woman who will be the mother of your children. I pray to God that this will be possible. I never want to leave you my dearest Steve.

So, let's put aside these dark thoughts. I'm going to be your wife, so don't try to get out of it! I love you Steve. Your letter today was beautiful. I love and need you so very, very much. I feel that no one shares the kind of love we share. Goodnight for now darling. Love, Your Brent.

May 11, 1964: Dearest Steve, You know Darling, I have been thinking about our house and about you and me in it. I see a really nice house with a nice lawn that leads to a nice little sandy beach, that is all our own. I happen to see myself waiting there for you to come home from work. I was doing the washing in our nice washer and dryer. In the summer I might hang a few things outside to dry. I see our "electric" stove, and your supper is ready. I even thought about maybe picking you up at work sometimes and of us driving home together. I want to look nice for you when you come home to me.

I also see some woodland around us. That is where our insurance for the future is growing—maybe for the children's education too. No kidding Hon, I really think I'm going to love keeping house for us. Do you know how deliriously happy I'm going to be keeping our own home. Oh boy! It will be wonderful to be able to clean every little corner of it.

The neighbors I haven't seen yet. I know they won't be too close, but I suppose they will be somewhere nearby in our country setting. However, I do see my brother and family; plus our parents, on both sides, coming to visit us. Maybe we can have Christmas or Thanksgiving at our house.

You know Hon, I want our home to have a little flare to it, but I want it to be very homey too. Maybe Darling, next year at this time, we may be able to start seriously looking for "our" house. I know it will depend on the job you get and where we go. However, we can dream forever!

I love you Mr. Martin, and I want you to tell me what you see for the future. I see so much happiness that it makes me happy now just to think about it. You had better watch out for me this weekend. I'm apt to try to smother you with love. Do you think you can stand it? I know I can. Will you smother me with love also, sir? Love, Brent.

May 13, 1964: Dearest Brent, I am in a mood for a talk to my Kitten tonight, and I am very glad you are talking to me Kitten about your ideas. So far they have been just the same as mine. (All but that darn electric stove! I have to improve my argument for a gas stove.)

Have you thought about using different kinds of wood flooring in different rooms? By doing this we could use oak, a very durable wood in the areas where there is a lot of wear and tear, and use pine in the areas we want to dress up. I like the idea of using colonial maple furniture, and one thing I demand for my den is a nice desk and a big armchair. If we get an old farm house, I might be lucky enough to get a fireplace in it. I see in my mind's eye a very nice place to plan hunting and fishing trips and to make love to my wife.

It may take a life time to reach some of our dreams Kitten; but, just having you beside me will make these years very happy. That is, if God wills our dreams to come true. When you marry me Kitten, he will have granted my most precious dream; the rest cannot help but follow.

There are so many things I want to talk to you about. What kind of flowers are we going to have in our garden? Do you want a lilac bush by one corner of our house? I can tell you one thing! We are going to have one garden devoted to nothing but roses! Then, of course, we are going to have a small vegetable garden. I suppose we will have a little trouble with deer getting into it.

I cannot wait to teach our son how to hunt and fish, to play baseball, and most importantly, during the passage of time, watch him grow into a man. Darling, you must somehow teach our daughter to be a woman as much as her mother is. Our children will be individuals. They do not have any form or shape they must live up to, but I want them to know how to work, love, and to be happy.

I had better get on the ball and look into graduate school pretty soon. If I do go to grad school, I will have to look into a loan or grant of some sort. I would really like to go if I can swing it.

I would have to enter the Forestry School, but I would like to pick up the rest of my credits necessary for my accredited degree in wildlife first. If I did that another year it would give me my master's degree in wildlife as well as forestry. We will have to talk the whole thing over.

I miss you Kitten. I love you more than anyone will ever know. Steve.

May18, 1964: Dearest Steve, This is going to be short and sweet as I have a test and two finals to study for. I have really felt good today because I did well on my pharmacology test, and a patient sent me a compliment via another student. Wow! But most of all, I have a feeling of being very, very close to you.

I have every confidence in you too darling. I also feel that I have grown up a little more after this last weekend. I realize the power of our love, and I can understand the feelings of other young people who haven't had quite as strong convictions as ours are, combined. I thank God for as wonderful a guy as you darling. I believe you could look any temptation in the face and turn it down; if you felt it was not what you wanted for the time and place. You have a very strong personality Steve. I love you for this. I have no fears in facing the world with you. You know what is right, and come hell or high water, you will stand by what you know is right. Always be this way my darling. You will always profit from it.

I am glad things happened the way they have. It has given me great insight into life, and it has helped me to see why things should be in logical order. I never consider any experience as wasted. We learn from everything we do. I have learned a very beautiful lesson from our love darling.

I must admit you can put me on a cloud so high that I'm feeling no pain what-so-ever! I think I have touched a little corner of heaven with you. I do believe that love was made by God. Anything man-made could not be so beautiful.

Good night. I love you more than words can say. Thank you for being you. I feel we have crossed a big chasm on our way to knowing each other. Love, your Brent.

P.S. Looks like I get to stay here. My advisor/instructor talked with me for an hour and a half. I have the goal of going to my obstetric, pediatric, and psychiatric affiliations in the near future! Love, Brent.

June 1, 1964: Darling Steve, Sir, I miss you like I've never missed anything before. If I don't see you soon, I shall go mad. I have a lot of choice little bits to tell you also. It was nice to receive such a long letter from you. However, it is almost completely mutilated by the repeated readings. That is what happens to letters when they are so few and far between.

I really hope you were able to conquer those exams though. Hail to the conquering hero! I'm going absolutely bats. I think I have done okay on my exams so far. I still have three more to go.

You know I want so much to feel your arms around me. I want so much to tell you how much I need you and love you. I ache just to be near you Darling. It seems like an eternity.

Darling, I am very glad you want to continue your education. I'm sure we will be able to work it out. I want so much to talk with you about all of these things again. It is so wonderful to be able to plan together.

Darling, I feel so lost. I need to come "home" very much. There is so very much I feel that I can't control myself. I feel terribly restless. I feel as though I am looking for something; and I know when I'm with you again, I'll be able to relax completely, because I will have found what I want so very much.

Our memories have really helped to make the last weeks bearable. We have the most beautiful things to remember. I love you Steve. See you soon Darling. I hope. Lady in distress. Love, your Brent.

June 2, 1964: Dearest Brent, I had my last final exam yesterday. Rich Wakefield and I came home with my grandparents, but we went back today with his Dad's truck to clean out our rooms. Also paid for summer camp, so that is off my mind.

In the last few days we have had all kinds of excitement here at home. On Saturday, a bear came out in the road just below our house. Dad and Mom watched it for a while until Dad put our dog Ty outside and set him on the bear. Dad ran out behind the house to the Lee's Mill bridges to watch the bear navigate the rocks and river as Ty put him across. But the bear decided to cross on the rocks Dad was standing on. Needless to say, the bear was rather scared when Dad yelled at him. We have not seen the bear since!

I miss you Kitten. I want to see you so very much. It seems like ages since I last saw those smiling eyes of yours. I need the relaxed feeling that you alone can give me. I want to hear you talk and laugh. I want to be near you Kitten. I love you Kitten.

I hope everything is going great with you Darling. Be sure to think of all the little things you have going around in that beautiful heard of yours. I know a guy that wants to hear every one of them. Good night Kitten, Steve

July 10, 1964: Dearest Brent I hope your day was a good one. Remember Kitten, you are working for our dreams right now. The work and the conditions under which you work are very difficult. But, are not our dreams worth even more work, if it was so required.

I am very happy and very proud of us Brent. We are doing very well for both ourselves and those about us. By getting our education we are making those about us happy, and we are at the same time making the fulfillment of our shared dreams much more certain.

Our life is ours alone to live Kitten. We will do our best to live our life as close to our ideals as possible. Our marriage can be very nearly perfect Kitten, but we are going to obtain this goal only if we live to satisfy the hungers within ourselves and not those that someone else has.

I have never tried to sell you a bill of goods, Brent. But now I am going to sell you some—our marriage! I cannot promise you the fulfillment of your dreams Kitten. I can only tell you that our dreams and desires are the same, and that I want to spend the rest of my life making you happy. I can promise you a chance to develop as a person and a chance to increase the scope of your interests. All I am saying Kitten is that I want to live my life instead of watching it drift away. My wife will have the same chance. As for our dreams Kitten, that they are wonderful dreams, there can be no doubt.

You and I are in a very good position to obtain at least some of them. Darn it Brent, I love you very much. No matter where we are or what we are doing, it will seem wonderful because you are there. So ends the case FOR our marriage.

If you have any reasons why we should not enjoy and make eternal the joy we have found in our love, KEEP THEM TO YOUR SELF!

Maybe I should not have added that last little bit to my "bill of goods." It kind of gives the wrong impression!

I have a lot to say to you Darling, but I think I will wait until Sunday. I love you Kitten. We can make our dreams come true. My biggest one came true the night I met you. I met an intelligent, yet beautiful girl, that one day would be my wife. Good night Darling. Here is wishing you the best of luck on the wards. Steve.

July 20, 1964: Dearest Brent, Good evening Darling. I hope your vacation is going nicely and that you are catching up on the sleep you missed at school.

Well Kitten, our first day of summer camp in the White Mountains of New Hampshire is nearly over. You must come up and see our "inn" sometime. It is very beautiful and peaceful here. Darling, it offers me everything I desire out of life, except for the most important thing: my Kitten.

You would not believe the pull you have on me Kitten. I cannot look at the moon or these beautiful mountains without missing you very much. Last night I watched our night sky long after most everyone else had gone to bed. Somehow, believing that you were looking at the same sky, it made me feel so very much closer to you. I am always close to you Kitten, but sometimes feeling close to you and not being able to touch you drives me slowly insane. It is really very beautiful up here Kitten. Just the same, I would enjoy this wonderful splendor about me much more if I was sharing it with you.

Well, now to tell you a little about camp. There are seventeen students and three instructors. Only the students stay here at the "inn." We hit the deck at 6:30 every morning. At seven we have breakfast. We make sandwiches for lunch right after breakfast and at eight classes start. Classes end at 4:30 p.m. every day. We are really off in the sticks here. We have no electrical outlets in our rooms and the only light is from an overhead light in every room.

We get our power from a small generator out back. At eleven every night the generator is turned off and with it, off goes all the lights. Every Wednesday we cut wood for the stove, pick berries for the pies we eat the rest of the week, and make old-fashion ice cream.

Phil and I have been set apart from the rest of the guys. We were told today that we, the Wildlife majors, were to have it quite a bit rougher than the strictly Forestry majors. Again, we take the Forestry courses and that little bit "extra" called Wildlife Management on top of that.

The head of camp this year appears to be really on the ball. I really have high hopes of getting something worthwhile out of this summer's work. From what I have seen of a few of the other guys is the general idea to just have a good time.

Well Darling, I realize I have not told you much about the whole affair, but I am saving the best until I see you. I miss you very much Kitten. I love and need you ever so much. Good night Kitten. Steve.

Much to Brent's delight, towards the end of Steve's summer camp, his parents invited her to join them on a visit to see him at camp. Brent was disappointed as the visit was much too short and allowed no time for Steve and her to have a private talk.

July 22, 1964: Dearest Steve, Here I am visiting my brother. We are at a Lake in Vermont, about a half hour from Wayne's farm in New Hampshire. We are waiting for a thunder storm to cease. I sure wish it would as the lightening is awful, and I hate these storms. I think my hair is standing on end, as it was so close, and I wish I was hiding in your arms. Some people think it is over and are now back in the water. Let them! I am so shaken by it I couldn't swim if I had to.

I hope you are getting a lot out of the Forestry Camp. I would hate to have you disappointed with it as our time together has been shortened by it this summer. We have a lot of memories all stored up for us, and I like to think about what we have done and about what we are going to do.

You know, I honestly believe we have something very special, and I don't know of anyone, unless it is your parents, who come anywhere near it. Love forever, your Brent.

July 23, 1964: Dearest Brent, I was very glad to hear from you. As far as camp being worthwhile, everything seems to be working out alright. As long as a person is willing to apply himself, he will get a lot out of this camp. One must really try to mess up to get a "D" out of the deal. Yet, the above average grades have been made correspondingly harder.

Phil and I should get something out of this summer. There are only the two of us Wildlife students, and we have two instructors. We have to complete a research project within the seven weeks of camp. We have a very good one planned, but more about it later. The summer has great potential.

I miss you Kitten. My love for you, and the world around me steady me day by day. Both are vital to my way of life; to the spirit within me. Good night Kitten, Steve.

August 4, 1964: Dearest Steve, I am back at the dorm, but I know where I'd prefer to be. That would be with you!

I must say I do not like the sound of the events in Vietnam. On the lighter side, I am already looking forward to seeing you Friday. Also, my first day on the Surgical Unit went well.

Another friend is feeling restless and feels like leaving training; as have several others from time to time. I wish I had another profession besides this one, the way she does! I would be with you so fast you wouldn't know what had happened.

I feel very inadequate when writing to you. I can't tell you how much I love you. I so want our life together Steve. It is something very special and something no one else can feel. Good night for now darling. See you soon, I hope and pray. Love, your Brent.

August 13, 1964: Dearest Steve, Hello darling. This is your crazy, mixed up girlfriend writing again. I am capable of getting so mixed up that I don't know which way to go. Some days it seems I can't stand this work any longer.

I suppose I have to confess to you. I did tell you about my talk with one of my instructors about a month ago. Well, for some reason I got going again last night. It is really so awful. I spent the day with a friend as I had told you. I came back to the dorm and it seemed so overwhelming. I decided it was foolish to stay by myself, so I went up the hall to talk with her again. Well, the school's administrator came through checking that everyone was in, and she told Liz it was time for lights out. So, I left and went down to my room. The administrator asked Liz what was bothering me; and she then came down and talked with me for a while.

I wish I could figure myself out. I guess things are beginning to take their toll. I'll just have to fight every time I feel this way. I want to talk with you about all of this. I really don't want to upset you. I'm okay, I guess. It is just I feel so trapped at times. I wish I could honestly say I like this work. There are so many things that are bothering me. I guess the best way to explain it is to talk with you face to face.

I miss you very much Steve. I want our life together so very much. I am afraid at times that I may be a disappointment to you. Please have faith in me, and try to understand me. I know it must be hard, because I don't understand myself. I do know I love you very much. I want to come home so very much, Good night Steve. Love, your Brent.

August 1964: Publicly, Brent wasn't ready to disclose the final blow that affected her decision to leave nursing school. Brent had inherited, from her maternal grandparents, enough money that would have paid for her three years of nursing school.

At that time, children were not considered adults until they were twenty-one years old. Therefore, her father had access to her bank account. He had mentioned once before that he had taken out enough to pay for his license plates!

Late in the spring when he had picked her up from school, he told her how much more he had taken from her bank account. She was speechless, as she had absolutely no recourse to recover the funds she needed to pay for the next two years; and students had already been told the tuition would be more than expected for the following year.

Upon returning to the dorm after the weekend, and after study hours were over, Brent went to confide in her friend the situation. Unaware that "lights out" time had come and gone, they were surprised when there was a tap on the door.

Brent will never forget the kindness and understanding of this previously assumed stern instructor as she listened with concern and compassion.

Brent never really regretted the decision she made that night. Her life fell into place, step-by-step, over the years. The first big step was the one leading closer to Steve's and her wedding day!

Thanks to her brother, who sent her $10.00 a week for food, which provided for a lot of tomato soup, with bread and butter, she was able to stay trim.

And, thanks to her brother's in-laws loan, she was able to pay for the next step of her education. It would, step-by-step, eventually lead to a Bachelor's degree in Business Education, and a twenty-six year middle and high school teaching career.

August 25, 1964: Dearest Steve, It seems, so far, that everyone has taken my news well. It is rather had to explain, because there are several reasons why I left nursing. There is one thing I do know. I want you as my husband and our life together over and above everything else. I love and need you so very much.

I am getting information about business schools in the New England area and will let you know what develops.

Darling, things just have to work out for us. I'm counting on improving my skills, as quickly as possible, so as to have a job and help you. I want to be able to do something for us instead of being the one who you will have to wait for to finish school.

Darling, we have to be able to start our life together as soon as possible. Now I want to plan to be ready to come to you as soon as you can possibly have me. I want you to have the best opportunity to pick the job you want, wherever you want, without having to think that I won't be there; because Darling, I'm going to be there now! Remember I love you. Your Kitten, Brent.

September 22, 1964: From Portland Maine, Dearest Steve, Hello my darling. I have good news, as I may be coming home every other weekend. I have figured it out, and if I come home next weekend (Oct. 2nd to 4th), I'll hit all the big weekends.

Actually, I love it here where I am living in a house on a cliff, overlooking the ocean; but three of us may move to an apartment in town. It may be cheaper. We will see. Another girl and I went out on the cliff and got sprayed by the surf churning up from the hurricane.

I have so much to tell you, and I am so glad I'm going to see you soon. So far, I am eating quite inexpensively. (It was actually tomato soup with bread and butter every night.) I hope school is going alright with you. Please take good care of yourself.

The school here is fine. However, it sure takes practice to achieve goals. Good night for now darling. I love you very much. Brent.

September 28, 1964: Dearest Kitten, Good evening Kitten. I hope everything is going perfectly for you. I am very glad to hear that you are so taken with Portland and the entire scope of happenings there.

Registration was the usual mess here, but we all managed to get the courses we wanted. This is really going to be a tough semester. All but one of my courses have graduate standing. I have really got to get on the ball. By the way, Phil and I finally got a wildlife course. It looks like "65" is going to be my year.

If you are able to come home this weekend, I will try to see you Saturday night. That is, if you will let me in the door. Good night Kitten. I have got a few things to tell you too! Love, Steve.

October 20,1964: Dearest Steve, good evening darling. I should be very happy tonight, but, oh do I ever miss you. I won't be able to come home this weekend. It seems, between our various commitments, we are apart for a while.

I hope you had a good time last weekend on Swan Island, as I hear it is a very nice place. Please, when you write, tell me more about it.

Darling, I saw Billy Graham tonight at City Hall. Bonnie Holmes and my cousin went with me. It was a nice service and there was quite a large crowd, but we did get seats. I wish you could have been with me as it was a rewarding experience.

Oh Steve, I want to see you so much! I miss you! All the things that have happened, and I want to share them with you.

Please take good care of yourself as I love you so much. I'll be so very glad when we can finally come "home" for good. Now look, I'm getting all upset over nothing. We have it made don't we, and the time is getting shorter.

Good night darling. Your Kitten is about to curl up and go to sleep. Good night Steve. Love, Brent.

November 2, 1964: Hi Hon. Good evening Darling. I hope you made it back to Portland in good shape last night. I did not get back to college until midnight.

I am really sorry about our misunderstanding last Friday night. Being away from you for any length of time really ties me up inside. I miss you so very much I am sometimes afraid of my dependence upon you; and so I have to show myself that I am independent. We can forget that Kitten. We have reminded each other just what a wonderful thing we share. It is too wonderful to be hurt by such a thing as false pride and the wild ideas people in love get when they are separated. So more than enough of that; the future is much too beautiful.

Someday very soon I am going to marry a very wonderful girl. This girl is the most important thing in the world to me. She is a very wild and beautiful thing, like those night skies I so enjoy watching. In both images I get such a feeling of dept and eternal beauty. I just have to be a part of both. You are something to watch, wonder at, and to love. I can do no more or less than any other guy. I can but give you all that I have and love you the way one worships the most important thing in his existence.

I ask you only to love and respect me, Kitten. Not very much to many people, but to me these things are all important. If I cannot give you the feeling resulting from these things, I am not fulfilling my ideas of what love is.

A person must give completely of himself in return for complete love; to really taste the fruit of the most widely sought tree in all of creation. The giving of complete love in return for a like gift, is the beginning of a series that is one of God's greatest gifts. It is so simple, yet, it is so hard to do. Do not think of yourself, but give of yourself. That is when you give of the true beauty that a human being is allowed.

I am still a boy Kitten. Yet, I have the body and needs of a man. Sometimes I feel as if I am being torn to pieces inside. I have come too close to making you mine, Kitten. It is time I started earning that respect that is so important to me. It is my responsibility, and I am going to treat it as such. I love and need you so very much Kitten. Not too much longer, and I will be asking you to come home. ALL THE WAY HOME!! Love, Steve.

November 9, 1964: Dearest Steve, I was sorry we were not able to see each other Sunday. Let's hope all our bad luck in now and not later.

Steve, you were the sweetest, most wonderful guy Saturday night. I love you that way. I love you any way, but that "way" is really something! I don't know how I was ever so lucky as to find and have such a wonderful man as you for my future husband. I am most thankful.

There are so many things I feel, that I would love to tell you. There never seems to be enough time left to be with you as much as I want to be. I love you very much, Steve. I admire you so very much. You are everything any girl would be glad to have. I am so lucky!

I hope you are able to replace the papers, etc. that you lost. Please get the driver's license replaced. There is only about one other "license" as important as your driver's license. Right?!

I will let you think about that for a while!

You know Darling, when we are home again I don't think I will let you out of my sight. I miss you so very much. I feel as though a very important part of my existence is not with me. I need you Darling. So good night for now. I love you more than words can say. Love, Brent.

November 15, 1964: Dearest Steve, Darling, it is so wonderful to be so sure of our love. The girls here are all finding their guys, and they wonder about this and that. I only sit back and feel so happy I could explode. It is so wonderful to have you, to know you love me and to know I love you completely; without any doubts what so ever. We have really been blessed with a most wonderful gift—the gift of true love.

I was a good girl yesterday, as I filled out those Bible study question sheets I got at the Billy Graham Crusade. They might really come in handy if I ever get back to teaching Sunday School again. I shall probably have another stint of it when our children are old enough to go to Sunday School.

I hope you had a good time on your trip this weekend. I had a quiet weekend. I did go down on the rocks by the ocean yesterday afternoon for a while. It was a beautiful day with a lot of birds around. I need you to identify some of them for me. I think about you all the time. We have so very much ahead of us. Good night. Love, Brent.

November 16, 1964: Dearest Brent, Thank you very much for the cake and coming to see me on my belated twenty-first birthday. I really don't know why you hang around with a guy like me. Must be you enjoy the mixed up way I do things.

Well Kitten, now that I have cried upon your shoulder and felt sorry for myself, I will tell you about the really very good things that have happened. This last Friday was a very eventful day. To start the day I really messed up a Forestry Management assignment. (Completely my fault.) That my dear lady is the first step upon the long road back; realizing just whose fault for such a disaster is and then openly admitting it.

This last Saturday we spent on a deer checking station in Vermont; and Sunday we were at the Kilkenny deer yard in New Hampshire, checking hunters and deer. There were 220 hunters in the yard. So you see, I had a really good time and learned quite a bit.

I have really go a lot to talk with you about. More dreams and grand hopes, but very worthwhile ones. I hope this letter finds you happy Kitten. I know I am Happy to be talking with you again. Forgive my silence last week, but things were kind of hectic and my company was not suited for the likes of you at that time. Besides, I get afraid of breaking something as small and as soft as you, while I am like that.

See you soon Beautiful. I will be in the long line of wolves outside your door. Maybe this next weekend you will take me in for a while, if I promise to be good. I love you Brent. Goodnight Kitten, Steve.

G
O
A
L
S

A
C
H
I
E
V
E
D

Chapter 5

Goals Achieved

January 5, 1965: Dearest Brent, Good afternoon Kitten. I hope school is going alright. Get those final courses done, and get out there, and start earning lots of money. Yay! Yay!

It looks like Rhode Island is the target this coming weekend, Brent. Our professor is trying to arrange rooms for us at the university there. As it stands now Kitten, I will not be home until February third.

It has been only three days since I last saw you, Darling. What I wouldn't give to see you again right now. I am thinking of you while I should be studying. I just decided I will take a post-graduate course in studying you; if you will permit me to do so. I think you should know that I am a very poor student. It will, no doubt, take me take rest of my life to complete a worthwhile study of such an interesting and variable topic as you are.

I love you very much Kitten. Thank you for being such a wonderful and lovely woman. Right now that particular combination is driving me slightly crazy. Someday, I promise, it will drive you crazy. Better get your track shoes out and go into some serious training. Good night Darling, Steve.

January 7, 1965: Dearest Brent, I hope you are having fun, Brent. Life is hard at times, yet it gives anyone willing to go half way many a good laugh. Believe me, Brent; I can have one hell of a good time just taking a close look at myself and my personality. People are really so very pitifully frail with their egos and inhibitions. With one eye upon our self-image, and the other upon our public image, no wonder we tear ourselves apart inside. We find it very hard to accept one half of ourselves; so we usually present to the world a shell that we consider the best we can offer of our inner most self, without hurting that image. In reality, which are we? One or the other? A combination? Or, maybe neither? Does it depend upon the individual?

Do you know who you are? Why were you put here? Why do you have the talents that you do? Why are you put together the way you are? Somewhere there must be a reason for our particular existence. Are we fulfilling our purpose? We cannot, unless we are giving life our all, can we?

Brent, I love you. Have a good time and study hard. Good night Darling. Steve.

January 11, 1965: Dearest Steve, Thank you for the letters. They mean a lot. I like to know what you are thinking in that great mind of yours and about what you are doing. I hope your trip this weekend was well worth it for the learning experience. For you, I'm glad about these trips; but as far as seeing you—it hurts! So, February third is your next time home. I hope I'll be able to be home then. At present I am finishing up my last business course. I have enjoyed the courses, and I am sure you are glad Business School suits me.

So, your finals are bearing down upon you. Darling, don't kill yourself over them. I am sure you will do very well. I have every confidence in you. By the way! I love the sound of your post-graduate course!

It really is something when one finally reaches the point where he or she faces the world and has to sell themselves and their talents. It sobers one a lot.

Remember, wherever you go, I shall follow. I won't alter your work. You, if anyone, alters mine; and that is ok. Furthermore, we will probably be having a family before too long after we are married. We will work it in, O.K.?!

Like you have ordered, my dear man, I am trying to have fun. Jan is a million laughs, and Nancy sobers me up; so it is an even keel I'm on, believe it or not.

I miss you very much. February third is a long way ahead. I hope I'm all settled somewhere by then. I will have so much to talk with you about. Good night my love. Take care of yourself. Love, Brent.

January 26, 1965: Dearest Steve, I want to get married! If it was at all possible right now, I'd marry you so fast you wouldn't know what hit you. I miss you very much. I love you more than anyone or any other thing in this world. I want to be your wife so very much. I want "us" together in our home. I want to plan with you and work with you. I want you where I know every morning that you will be home again at night.

Steve, nothing means as much until I can share it with you. There is no plan or future unless I have you to share it with for always. No matter what I ever do, I'll always love you. You are the only person to whom I can give my whole self. I love you Mr. Martin. See you before too long. Love, Brent.

February 16, 1965: Dearest Brent, Good evening Darling. I hope work went well for you today. Seems a bit strange does it not? The day we have waited for so long is rapidly approaching. In a little while you will become my wife. You are very rapidly losing your last chance to back out Kitten. Once your name becomes the same as mine you will have to put up with me and my ways the rest of your life. We have been married in a good many ways for a long time Kitten. This gives me a great deal of faith in us Kitten. We have proven by this, and countless other ways, that we truly love each other, and cherish the relationship that has grown and flourished between us.

I know your presence has helped me a great deal Brent. I only hope I have given you the same feeling of security, and of being loved and needed, as you have given me. Our love has proved itself more than a marriage of hearts, but of spirits as well.

I love you very much Brent. We are both giving up some of our dreams in order that your name might be changed to "Mrs. Martin" in the near future. I feel that it is worth a hundred times any dream I ever had. To be able to provide for you, share life with you, and love you as my wife for the rest of my life, seems in itself, a wonderful dream that is always just out of reach. I do not know if I can stand waiting so long for you to come home, Kitten. I love you very much. The woman I love very much about to become my wife. Can you imagine! I know you are what I have always dreamed my wife had to be. But not only am I allowed to know you, but to also have your love, and on top of all this, you are to be my bride. Good night, Kitten. Steve.

February 16, 1965: Dearest Steve, My job at the insurance company is going well, and the greatest ever was when I was given my first paycheck today! It was a little more than what I had expected it to be. It was sure burning a hole in my pocket on the way home. I haven't decided which bank to put it in yet.

I miss you very much. I hope your rugged schedule isn't getting you down. You know Sir, I love you very much. And, by the way everyone thinks your Valentine cards are great. Thank you so much for them and for a wonderful weekend!

You know you have a definite fan club as far as my father is concerned. He thinks you are quite a guy. I shall have to tell you about how funny he can be at times. He can be okay now and then! I must close for now. Please continue to write often. I have to hear from you. Good night darling. Love, Brent.

February 28, 1965: Dear Brent, I hope you will forgive the long silence from this quarter, Brent. Things have been particularly rushed these last few weeks.

I am pleased to hear that your work is going well. Speaking of jobs, I am planning to apply to The Bureau of Land Management for a job as a forester in Alaska. I am also going to try the Forest Service, Bureau of Indian Affairs, and the Fish and Wildlife Service.

Someday, I want my own land. A place I can live quietly with my wife and start something that I can pass on to my son. I pray he will have the same feelings when he sees the wild things about him growing and replacing themselves. Then someday, he will realize that as long as he can see and remember these things, he too, will be just as free as the things he sees about him.

Enough of my garbled thoughts and my wishes for this and that. Leave it to me. Is not talking about yourself one the basic "do not's!"

I hope you are having fun Brent. The group you go with sounds very nice and a lot of fun to be with. Love, Steve.

March 4 1965: Dearest Steve, You don't know how glad I am to finally hear from you. I miss your presence when you aren't continually there. I know you are in thought, but it is so nice to have something tangible.

I'm glad you are finding job possibilities. Look them over and take what you think is best for you. There are so many things for us to discuss and do. However, at present we just have to wait. Sometimes it makes one feel helpless.

About my job. I like it very much, and I don't know how I was so lucky to find it. The people I work with are really the best.

The work is varied, quite interesting, and there is never a dull moment. I have taken over quite a lot of work from the other three ladies in my section. In time I will probably have more.

My transportation source to get home has a change in schedule. So now I have to budget my weekends home. I plan to go home only if I know for sure you plan to be there too. Take care of yourself Darling. I love you, Brent.

March 14, 1965: Dearest Brent, Good evening. When I write tomorrow night, I should have a very good idea of how things stand here at the University regarding changes in the curriculum to fulfill graduation requirements. This thing has really got me all mixed up inside. It can take a year right out of my life. A year that I have had a great many hopes and dreams about for a long while. My parents refuse to believe that I could be put in such a situation that I might not be able to get my degree in June, due to a sudden change in course requirements!

That is why I am talking to you about the whole thing, Kitten. It always helps to talk to someone you know is interested.

Kitten, I love you so very much. We have special likes and dislikes, ideals, and dreams the same as every other person in this world. These are the things that separate man from the rest of the animals. Man is a curious creature, and he is a free moral agent. In other words, he has the choice of doing what his ideals demand and what he believes to be right, or letting these beliefs slip between his fingers. Like water that falls upon parched earth, these beliefs once lost are difficult, if not impossible to retrieve. It is so easy to simply exist and fulfill the simple ecological functions of an animal; but it is difficult to go against public opinion or established norms. You live life by doing so, if your ideals and beliefs demand it.

Kitten, no matter whatever happens, always be secure in your knowledge that you have brought into an average guy's life a dept of feeling, and a touch of eternal spring he would never have hoped to experience otherwise. I will never regret having known you, laughed with you, or having fallen in love with you. It will always remain an untouchable ideal; something every guy wants, and so very few deserve.

Damn you Kitten, I can no longer be happy alone in the woods ever. You manage to chase me everywhere; there is no escaping you. After taking a perfectly happy guy and slowly pressing upon his every thought, until he can think of only you. Why that is a perfect example of thought and emotional kidnapping. My lawyer informs me that this case will be an absolute breeze in any court in the land. So you might as well give up and marry me. No matter how nervous it makes you. You had better because I am prepared to fight it to the highest court in the land, if necessary.

Good night Kitten. Take care of yourself and work hard. Come home as soon as possible, Brent. I need the woman that is Brent. I need her very much, and I will fight like hell to make her my wife. Love, Steve.

March 17, 1965: Dearest Brent, Well Kitten, tomorrow morning we get the news, good or bad about the changes in the graduation course requirements to graduate with a dual degree in Forestry and Wildlife. The faculty voted upon our case this afternoon. We think the decision will be close, no matter which way it goes. They have been good enough to tell us that we can read a protection book and then take an exam, which if we pass gets us our Forestry degree. However, there are a couple of slight catches to this little deal. It will cost us extra for the three credit course; and without lecture notes, there is a very good chance of getting a low grade on the exam.

If I can't graduate this June, I will keep returning until I have received my degree. I have not hidden my feelings concerning this situation to anyone I have talked to. In fact, I could very well have hurt our cause by blowing up in the face of the professor responsible. After a few words about him and the Forestry Department in general; I did have sense enough to shut up. Phil tried to smooth things over as much as possible. I hope the professor did get the idea that I was holding him responsible, despite his efforts to imply that we were trying to sneak out of something.

I have set my sights on something: either I fly high, or I do not fly at all. I truly feel that I am right, and that I am being taken advantage of. Men are very small and weak things; the only strength within them are their ideals and beliefs. I would not deserve what I believe the degree gives me, if I could only see the now; and let an over developed sense of pride keep me from reaching it. By the same token, I can't give up everything I hold that are my rights and ideals; nothing in the world is worth half of that.

My standards are strange to many people, maybe even to you. To these people I will always be an outsider because I am different from what their standards say I should be. However, I would rather be a stranger and an outsider to them, than to myself.

I need your warmth, strength, and sweetness today and for all the tomorrows allotted us. Yet, even something as wonderful as this would be found lacking if I could not give to you. Good night Kitten. I love you very much. Please come home to me soon, Kitten. You are the highest heights I will ever test my wings to reach. Love, Steve.

March 22, 1965: Dearest Brent, Good evening Brent. It was very nice hearing your voice tonight. I will never be able to tell you how much it means to me to have you beside me. A few soft words from the right woman can make a guy feel awfully tall. Right now despite my temporary troubles, I am very glad that I am young and that my woman can make me feel tall enough to reach the star our dreams are pinned to.

Tomorrow we go and see the Dean of the School of Agriculture. Phil and I have decided to cause as much trouble as possible. We have no idea that it will help our situation what-so-ever; but maybe someone else will not get the raw deal we feel we did.

Good afternoon Brent. Well, we have been to see the Dean. It seems that we lack nine credits necessary to graduate under the general studies program. As usual, the Forestry Department threw us into a situation before they looked.

The Dean told us that he had been told that the entire problem resulted when we tried to sneak out of taking some tough credits. Guess what we told him! He got mad enough to say that he was going back over to the Forestry Department and tell them to think it over and come up with another decision. No one knows where anyone stands right now, least of all Phil and I.

As things stand now, I will either graduate this June with a Bachelor of Science degree in Forestry, or I will come back next fall and pick up the necessary credits for the Wildlife degree. I will not be enlisting in the service this summer as things now stand. Damn them Brent, I am getting that degree! It has been a long while since I have been this mad. I have been quiet too long I guess. Well now, I am in a fight, so I guess I might as well fight.

Well Kitten, enough of the funny curves life somehow manages to throw everyone. I feel like talking about some very beautiful curves that belong to a very special woman. Talk about them? God, what I would not give to be holding them right now. Did you know I turn very soft inside and full of love whenever I see or think of you. I have been looking for you for what seems to have been a long while, Brent. I possess you to a degree I do not believe you realize Kitten.

Or, maybe it is you that so completely possesses me. I really do not know. The important thing to me is that you are never far from me. I constantly see your beauty reflected in the beautiful things about me. The wind whispers your soft love words and laughter in my ear, the ocean in its endless motion reflects your own throbbing vitality and love of life; and the stars in the cold night sky are so much like the warmth, strength, and purity of feeling and emotion I have found in you.

You have given this guy more warmth and happiness than he ever hoped for in his wildest dreams Kitten. To say that I do not want to make you completely mine would be a very big lie, Brent. I want to be able to love and support you the rest of your life. Remember, you have given me more love than I ever had a right to ask for. You have made me a very lucky guy Brent. Love, Steve

April 7, 1965: Dearest Steve, So you didn't recognize who was behind you Saturday night. We tooted three times for you. I hated to see you go in a different direction. I wish we were going the same direction. That time is getting closer.

Please let me know the date for your graduation. So glad everything has worked out for you and Phil. Please let me know the date for your graduation. I'll take my vacation then, regardless. I hope you are enjoying your vacation. I sure wish I was there with you. I miss you, Sir. I bet you are getting in a lot of hunting and fishing. Good night for now Darling. I love you. Brent.

April 9, 1965: Dearest Brent, Well, Kitten, I have good news for you. It seems that I will be having work both Saturdays and Sundays. My ring fund should really be swelling to its very limits before long. I have enough money to get through the rest of the school year. So, the money I earn weekends can go into the bank account and see us to a few dinners and outings. That had better sound as if I am seriously and honestly working towards our marriage. Darn it girl, I worked almost as hard to get you to fall in love with me and to want to share my dreams and hopes.

It is our love and understanding that makes us human. The wonderful thing that we found in each other's heart and arms is the most important thing in the world to both you and me. I love you Brent. I need you more than I even know. I want you to come home for good Brent. I want you for my wife.

You were wrong Brent. The other day we were not going in different directions, to different places maybe, but in the same direction. Both of us left to work towards our marriage. Now that is what I call direction!

By the way Kitten, I want to earn every cent of the money for your ring. No loans for something that means as much as this does.

Good night Kitten. I love and want you. I always will. See you soon. Love, Steve.

April 20, 1965: Dearest Brent, I miss you very much Kitten. It is unbelievable how nice it is to be close to you, even while we are apart. But at times it makes things quite hard. It is very hard to study or work when I am needing to touch and hold you so bad that I would give up the sun to bring you close to me for a moment.

Please always talk to me Brent, either while we are together or through our letters; but always talk to me. Do not be afraid to talk to me like you did last Friday. A guy always wants to hear the things you told me that day. I know I will always remember the words you said. They gave me a pride in myself and in us that no one else nor anything else could have. You have given so very much Kitten. Darn it Kitten, how in hell did I ever get a girl like you. It is too good to be true but it is the one dream I would never give up.

I hope you have called your brother and had a good talk with him about your father. Try to understand your father. People quite often lash out at those they love the most, when they feel they have failed.

I am not saying that you have not given him more love and understanding than anyone has the right to ask; but someone like him needs these things very badly. I know that you love him despite all the hardships. Kitten, we will always help them as much as possible. Good night Darling. Love, Steve

April 21, 1965: Dearest Steve, Good evening my darling. It was oh so nice to hear from you today.

Darling, I want you to go for your master's degree if you really want it. I'll go with you anywhere and help as much as I can. I am sure we can swing it. I have great faith in you even though I lack it in myself. There are so many things going for us, and we have every joy life has to offer. It is all within our grasp, isn't it Darling!

As you suggested, I had a talk with my brother about our father. He knows how difficult he can be and would help financially if he could. So, I will send financial aid now and then.

I must say good night for now. I love you. Good night, sweet dreams. Love, Brent.

April 26, 1965: My Dearest Steve, Tomorrow marks the second anniversary of our meeting each other. I truly believe that was the luckiest day of my life. So much has happened since then. Everything has worked to prove that you and I were truly meant to have and to hold each other. Like it has been said: "I could never find another you."

You say we have only had two real fights in the past two years. It is funny indeed. It seems that both things were something that each of us thought we could handle within ourselves. It took a lot of understanding for both of us to share these things. I would say that if the past is a promise of the future, that our future is sure to be the best!

By the way Sir, thank you for the card. You just keep me laughing. Don't worry, I'll get you yet! Ah ha!

I must say goodnight Darling. I love you Steve. I will see you Friday night, I hope. Shall we celebrate this weekend just by being with each other? I feel very full of happiness just thinking about you and our life together. Love, Brent.

May 11, 1965: Dearest Steve, It sure was awful leaving you Sunday night. I must say, however, I love it when you kiss me the way you did when you left. I plan to collect some more of those.

Say Darling! Shall we introduce our fathers at the wedding? Maybe in the reception line?! This is really funny. They haven't met yet!

Sue and I plan to come see you Tuesday night on campus. I hope your friend Peter Pohl can go with Sue. I am really looking forward to this. We will do whatever you guys want. Well, you know what I mean and don't mean! I love you! Brent.

June 4, 1965: Dearest Steve, You know Darling you made me very happy this weekend. I want our life together very much. There is no reason now for us to put it off much longer. I will be most proud to accept your ring. I think you have picked a lovely time to announce it. Darling, I hope your exams went well. Just think, my Steve is a college graduate; a man of his own now. He even wants to take care of me now. Everything we have hoped and waited for is now about to come to pass. How truly wonderful. I feel so happy when I think about it. I love you my Mr. Martin. Ours will be a beautiful life together. Good night darling. See you this weekend. I love you, Brent. (P.S. Enclosed is the information for you and the men to get measured for your wedding suits!)

June 9, 1965: Dearest Brent, Good evening Darling. Tonight I got some very good news that I want to share with you. A consulting forester, in the area, told my parents to have me call him, and he would help me locate a job.

I called him tonight to hear what he thought. After spending about ten minutes talking about my qualifications, he hired me. As it stands now, I will work with him and a couple other consulting foresters.

He believes that I will be plenty busy. The job will also give me the opportunity to get practical experience and to look around for something better with more room for advancement. The wage is enough to pay my way and that of my family. It will give us a good running start on our future.

Ask me about our car sometime Kitten. Something else that has worked out very lucky for us, and I am very elated tonight Kitten.

To be truthful I am very thankful to have the waiting and wondering behind me. I was going slightly bats with the vagueness of it all. Now I can enjoy the rest of my vacation.

I am also very much in love with a certain young lady. Boy, have I a lot to talk to her about. Love, Steve.

June 22, 1965: Dearest Brent, I started work last Monday. So far I enjoy it very much. Did you know I am crazy? Just two days on the job, and already I have my eye on the bosses job.

He runs the transit, and boy, I want to do that. Once I can do that, I can go on my own.

Our car is on the road now, and wait until you are in it. Boy, you will not believe this one.

Everyone sends their love. By the way Kitten, some "Joe" I know loves you very much. You give him the strength to live life, not wish he did. It is your name he whispers aloud at night. It is for you that he feels a passion and yet a purity of love that he has ceased to question, but now merely recognizes as a part of himself. As much a part of him as his pride in his name, himself, and you.

It is your voice and arms he cries out for when desire breaks over him like the waves of a stormy sea. It is your beauty he sees all about him, constantly reminding him of you. It is your words, arms, and love that he will spend the rest of his life earning. What he would not give to feel your arms about him and breath upon his face. He wants to hold you the rest of his life, if only in his heart. Maybe you will hold him there in your heart also. Love, Steve.

June 22, 1965: Dearest Steve, Good evening Mr. Steven Martin with that "B.S. "after your name! It is good to hear that things are going well for you.

By the way, where were you during motor cycle weekend when the riots hit Laconia? What a thing to happen during this annual event! I was really surprised to hear about it on the radio. I am waiting for your version and opinion.

I am so looking forward to coming home soon. Good night. Yours forever, Brent.

N

In the late summer and the early autumn of 1965 there were no more letters between Steve and Brent. Brent had come home to marry Steve!

On October 2, 1965, at 2:00 p.m. Steve and Brent were married at the Melvin Village church. The church was full of family and friends. Two friends from nursing school participated in the ceremony. Liz was a brides maid along with Brent's sisters-in-law. Bonnie Plummer Holmes's sweet voice filled the church singing a beautiful rendition of a current popular love song.

Brent remembers walking down the aisle with her father, and the rest was a blur. As would be expected, there are memoires captured in pictures of that wonderful day with Steve, looking totally handsome in his groom's suit and her in the wedding dress she had made to wear for him.

And yes, Steve remembered, and surprised her for their honeymoon by taking her to Lancaster County, Pennsylvania; as she had dreamed about in a letter to him in 1964. It was her first trip south, out of New England. It would not be long before their life would take them even farther south.

Steve and Brent returned to his parent's home for a couple of weeks after the honeymoon. Steve was keeping something from Brent. He was very much aware of the military draft, and that he would probably be drafted anytime.

Steve located a house to rent in another town, and they moved into their first home together. The single bedroom house was newly build; and, they loved furnishing it with wedding gifts and furniture from her parents. They also adopted a black and white Springer Spaniel puppy and a darling black and white kitten. Brent has a vivid memory of the evenings when Steve would work at his desk on their budget and make lists of what they hoped to purchase for their home in the future. They were together in the house for only three months.

Brent does not remember any discussion about Steve enlisting. He, however, determined that he would choose his own service, had completed the paperwork and had chosen the United States Marine Corp. The draft letter did arrive, and he notified the draft board that he had enlisted.

The landlord was notified, and much to his disgruntlement with having his tenants leave so soon, agreed on a final rental payment. After Steve left for Officer's Candidate School, Brent's father helped her move back home. The puppy went to live with Steve's parents, and the kitten went home with Brent.

They were separated again. Letters to Steve were addressed to:

Candidate Steven W. Martin, OCS, Quantico, VA

Hers were addressed: Mrs. Steven W. Martin, Wolfeboro, NH.

LIFE IN THE MILITARY

Chapter 6

Life In The Military

January 4, 1966: Dumfries, Virginia: Dearest Brent, Well Kitten, here I sit in a rented room sincerely wishing you were here. I am now as close to Quantico as I can get by bus. Tomorrow morningg morning I will take a cab onto the base.

I arrived here at about half past ten this forenoon. You really move right along on those buses. I took a Trailways bus all the way to Washington, D.C. There, I had to switch to a Greyhound bus. The longest wait I had was an hour in Boston. In New York City and Washington it took about a half-hour. The trip through Boston and New York city was made entirely in darkness; yet neither impressed me as a good place to live. I would like to go shopping there, as I know you would too.

Washington appeared really quite different. Naturally, there were plenty of impressive Federal buildings to improve the overall image. It appears quite well laid out with particular notice being given to making the city appear spacious and airy. Quite a change from the cramped and crowded quarters of New Your City and Boston.

Virginia, at least the part I have seen, can be given back to the Indians. It seems drab and dull looking without mountains and the large tracts of dark green evergreens of New Hampshire hillsides. I think half of this feeling is due to the difficult time I had in finding a room.

In case I am not able to reach the folks, please tell them that everything is fine; but, I could not get the call through. I have already tried twice. I am going to try once more before calling it a day. I sure hope you are there when I call.

For goodness sake Brent, keep busy. Now is your chance to expand without the "Old Man" hanging over you. Please limit the expansion to your interest and skills, not your waistline!

I love you very much Kitten. I sure do miss you. As you probably guessed, I do not like long good-byes. I guess you must really be my wife because it was you it really bothered me to leave. You just wait! Good night now Kitten. Take good care of yourself. With all my love, Steve.

January 6, 1966: Dear Kitten, Well Brent, we are getting cold, rainy weather here in the "sunny" south. I had another flight physical this morning and two cavities filled by a Dr. "Cheney."

I will not give you my address until early next week. We are being moved, once the main group of candidates arrive Monday. Do not try to send mail until you get my entire address. By the way, inform everyone: NO FOOD if you want me to remain at all friendly. I am not kidding!

Today we were issued our uniforms complete with a "Candidate haircut." Since you do not like me with short hair, Honey; you had better not take a close look at me for two or three years.

Our Company area is hard on a series of railroad tracks. The darn railroad company has not heard that railways are slowing down on business. It seems that a train goes by every fifteen minutes, not only that, they blow their horn and ring the bell.

Tonight I am on fire watch for two hours. Please keep yourself busy; this will be over in ten weeks. (I hope!) I am glad I had a good idea of what this entire thing would amount to.

I hope Dad and Mom from both sides of the family are alright. Please tell them that everything is fine with me. Take it easy Kitten. Be my girl now and always. You do not know how much I need this. With all my love. Good night darling, Steve.

January 8, 1966 Lee's Mill, Martin Home: Dearest Steve, Everyone was so glad to get a chance to read your letter. Your Mother didn't read the last page as she said that was for me!

Today is a day you would love. It has been snowing all day and there is quite an accumulation. The roads are slippery. I spent last Monday and Tuesday nights with your folks. Wednesday night I stayed at the Wolfeboro house. Thursday I moved everything out. What a job that was!

Dad filled the truck, and I made two trips with the car. It snowed that afternoon also. Thursday I stayed with my parents. Last night I came up here with your letter and our dog, Missy. I guess I'll stay put as the storm is as before.

Your folks and I had lunch with the Grandparents Martin. Grammie says you write wonderful letters. "That Steve is so deep; his thoughts, etc. He sees so much in everything!"

I can't wait to hear from you again. I want to know all about everything that has happened to you. Now don't soften things up, say as they are!

By the way, instruct me please, on what to do with our income taxes.

The Tollow family said hello to you. When we said good-bye she called me "dear" and shook my hand. I thought she was about to cry.

Darling, I miss you very much. It will be so wonderful to see you again. This will all be worthwhile if it allows us to be together again soon. It is still hard to imagine two and one-half months must pass. I'd be so glad to see you now that I can't imagine what it will be like then. I love you, my husband.

I will close for now but will continue later. I hope I get your address soon. This letter does you no good just sitting here. Missy doggie says hello and that she misses you too! Love, Brent.

January 9, 1966: Hello darling Steve. What a storm! There is a foot of snow everywhere. The car had a problem starting today. My Dad plans to take it to the garage to see if anything can be done to improve it. Maybe a new battery?

I spent the weekend at your parents. I was going to stay only Friday night, but I stayed longer because of the storm.

I have a surprise for you. At least, I hope it is or will be. Today, I started an 8" by 10" painting! I bet you don't believe me. Well, I did. It is of a covered bridge. So there. Actually, it looks quite amateurish right now. Your mother will help me improve it. It is fun when it looks anything like a bridge. It is in your room to dry so no one else sees it! What do you think of that? Love, Brent.

January 9, 1965 Quantico, VA: Dear Brent, I hope your parents and mine are alright. Tell them everything is okay with me. I am not getting rich, but maybe tomorrow. I am really concerned that everything is going fine with you. You are the only wife I've got, and I would like to keep you happy.

Boy, am I tired. What I would not give for twenty-four hours of sleep. That is what I am going to have to fight all the time I am here is being tired. I think I am slowly gaining on that little problem.

The weather is really cold down here. Today, the wind was blowing hard enough to knock a guy down. Marching is nice under these kind of conditions!

Monday, the rest of the candidates arrive. Thank God that we have four days experience under our belts. Things promise to be hectic starting Monday and will be for the next ten weeks. So, if you think I am not making much sense now, just wait. However, the chow here is good as long as you leave the potatoes alone. This morning we had a really good piece of steak to eat.

I have to get busy now, Honey. I will write again soon. Take care Kitten. I really do love you. Good night Darling, Steve.

January 10, 1966, Quantico, VA: Dear Brent, I am getting along alright, but I sure do miss you Honey. When I get home I plan to see a lot of you.

Everything is really different from civilian life. I think I have made the transition, so far, alright. You have to use every minute of every day to stay on top.

There are some rumors that we can get liberty the 17th of March. So, if we can swing it, maybe you can come down for my graduation. (I hope!)

All the former N.C.O.'s (Non Commissioned Officers) here think that the President will ask for an expansion of the war in Vietnam. There is no doubt where the majority of us will end up. It is still the place to do our fighting. Be that as it may; here I am, and I am going to do a good job. Everyone has to do something to get started on the road up.

Right now I would like to head right back to our little cottage; but, I will be darned if I am going to be an assistant carpenter all my life. Just like you do not want to do anything but sit around the house all day. One has got to get ahead.

We have to have various uniforms taken to the cleaners every day. We visit the barber every week. So, I will not send home very much, if any, of my first pay check.

Talk is that the Aviation Officer Candidates get thirty days leave before reporting to flight training. I would count on something quite a bit less.

Tomorrow we move to our permanent quarters. So you will be getting my address. You had better write! I consider that your part of helping strengthen your nation's security.

Hey, did you realize that you are my wife? You were amazed by the thought that I must provide for you no matter where I am, or what

I am doing. Well Honey, one beautiful day I am going to walk up to you, and I am going to receive just payment for every cent!

This is really a pretty select school, Kitten. There were only fourteen N.C.O.'s picked to attend this flight school. This is the only Officer Candidate School in the U. S. serving the Marine Corps. The reason we had to report early was to take another flight physical and to clear the company barracks area.

Two candidates were here in the last class. They dropped out because of broken legs, etc. Anyway, these candidates say 25 to 35 of the candidates are flunked out. I am going to have to go like the devil, Kitten. They do not just pass them by here. Either you learn or else. Dog-eat-dog; individual completion.

Don't worry Honey. I am going to make it. I love you Kitten. Better believe in me. Love, Steve.

January 15, 1966 Quantico, VA: Dear Brent, Good evening, Kitten. I want you to know I have laid aside my M14 just to write you. I have not had a chance to do anything, but run, for the last week. From 5:30 to 10:00 we go flat out.

Honey, this place will be the ruin of us money wise. I am going to have to save most of my first paycheck to pay for necessities. Before graduation, I have to purchase a winter service uniform that has to be ordered by the end of this coming week.

Hold onto your hat, my basic uniforms cost from $800.00 to $1,000.00. Talk about girls being particular about their clothes. The government will pay some of it, after graduation.

Well, now for the particulars. Most candidates last the ten weeks. During the last week everyone is evaluated by the staff. It has been known that 25% of a class has been cut. Needless to say everyone is going to have to go flat out. Each person is graded on leadership, physical conditioning, and academics. It is really going to be one hell of a ten weeks. I really do not know, Honey. Just go, go, and GO; and hope for the breaks.

Because I am tall, I have a squad of sixteen men under me now. So far, everything has gone well. It looks like I will have them for at least three weeks; if I do not screw up. A squad leader can find himself marching at the rear of the platoon because he messes up.

The physical training here is out of this world. The officers lead us in exercises, and they really run us into the ground. They keep an ambulance close by with its motor running during P.T. Guys have been known to fall flat on their faces during the daily runs or receive torn ligaments, etc. We got our first set of five shots, and boy, are those pressure guns the thing.

Well Honey, you know I miss you. You can't imagine the pleasure I get thinking about how you look and act. Lady I am going to look at you for hours when I finally get close to you.

I am really looking forward to seeing our chair that you are refurnishing. Keep yourself busy. I have to get busy again now, Honey. Nine weeks from now I am going to see the most lovely woman in the world, my woman. Good night Kitten. I will write tomorrow. Until then Honey, all my love. Love, Steve.

January 16, 1966, Quantico, VA: Dearest Brent, Good evening Darling. I hope everything is going well for you. I bet you sure look beautiful.

What I would not give to see you. Well, we have only nine weeks left before I do get to see you, what is more, get to hold you.

I hope you understand the lack of letters, Honey. You know I want to hear about things at home and how you are, but my time is unbelievable. I just do not get any free time. Things should be better next week. After seventeen hundred our time is our own. While I will still have to go like hell, I should be able to get a couple more letters sent per week.

Today, I have been straight out. At seven hundred I went on duty as corporal of the guard. By nine hundred I had made out liberty passes for about thirty men. My relief arrived half an hour late. After "brunch" another member of the platoon and I planted a couple of pine trees in front of the squad bay. That is what happens when the platoon commander learns you are a graduate forester. After that, I somehow managed to get picked to clean and dust the company commander's office.

The rest of the time I have spent getting ready for inspection tomorrow. Going to supper took up a half hour. On the weekends I really take my time to eat! It is now twenty-thirty, and I have made time to talk to my girl. You can't imagine how much I look forward to this.

Do you think that you could afford a long distance telephone call? I would sure like to hear your voice and to hear what you have been doing. Needless to say, I would like to call my parent's house. At seven hundred Sunday morning I will start trying to get you there. The lines for the phones are long and the phone lines between here and you are mixed up, so please be patient. If I do not hear from you before then, I will call.

Boy, do I love you Honey. At night I just lie in the rack thinking about you and those wonderful three months we shared. Girl, we were and continue to be really lucky. Keep yourself happy for us Kitten. My ego tells me that you will never regret it. Boy, that is one thing this program gives you. Either they make you an indecisive person or a super egoist.

I have to shower now Kitten. (You know, we never did take a shower together.) I will be seeing you soon. Keep busy, Honey. Get the most out of every day. Good night Kitten, Steve.

January 17, 1966: Hello Darling Steve. I haven't written for a week. I have been off galivanting. I'm glad I went this week because I still don't have your address! I now feel much more confident in going places by myself. I actually drove over to Portland and saw the girls and everyone at my former job. They all liked the pictures of the wedding. Everyone said "hello" to you and wished you the best of luck.

One neat thing happened. I met another girl with same first name as mine, which doesn't happen often. Her husband may be in Pensacola, FL next year. She worked at the same company in Portland that I did. She was so glad to meet me. I asked her if her husband was in the Marine Corps. She said: "Yes, is there any other service?" I said: "I get that viewpoint from my husband too!"

I'm glad to hear from you and that you are okay. I don't like the sounds of Vietnam!

Darling, did you know you addressed your second letter to Mrs. Brent "Cheney?" We thought, for sure, that they had really brain washed you! Remember you changed my name to "Martin!"

March 17th sure sounds great! I'm waiting for that day to come. I guess I have been doing quite well so far in keeping busy. I may drive up to see my brother next month. It is something to look forward to.

It seems like a century since you left. I know it will be great when we get together again! Love, Your Mrs. Brent Martin!

January 18, 1966, Quantico, VA: Dearest Brent. Good evening Honey. As you can see I have taken time again to talk things over with you. Actually, I got squared away in good shape before I sat down. I am now all showered, shaved, and I am writing to my girl!

Tonight I was fitted to a graduation uniform. A $135.00 worth of uniform. Thank God it is not a special one, but one worn every day.

Tuesday, the twenty-fifth of January, we are being flown to North Carolina to attend an air show at one of the Marine Air Stations there. At the end of the show we will be flown north again; about twelve hundred miles in one day. All the in an effort to gain more pilots. The word is that we are being flown down and back up in a C-130. In case you do not know that is one hell of a big cargo plane.

Out of the original forty-nine candidates, we are now down to forty-six. One is in sick bay with a bad leg and two more are trying to get out. These boys really arrived here in poor shape. Only one of us worked out for any length of time before hand.

The chow is good, and we get all we can eat. I would not be surprised if I put on a little weight. Everyone eats plenty of food, and nothing gets thrown away.

Tell the folks I am thinking of them: but, I just would not be able to write everyone I would like to with our present schedule. So, I am relying on you to pass the good word. I hope to get paid tomorrow. It will be nice to have a little change in one's pocket.

I hope you will not mind if I get personal now. Did you know I really and truly dream and think constantly about you. You really have no mercy for me, do you? I am really glad. I truly feel like a married man, a happily married man. Be mine now and forever, Honey. I can't tell you how much this means. Love, Steve.

January 19, 1966: Dear Kitten, Well Kitten, tonight we have only forty-three members of my platoon. A few guys can't make the grade. I hope later on it is not me. I know I am not leaving on my own accord. I am sticking.

Even the trains are still running on the nation's busiest railroad, once every half hour. They are challenging us to keep up the pace.

Next Saturday is our first personal inspection. It could be quite a shake down. A test will be this coming Monday, and the candidates will be taking over the platoon and company command posts. I drew squad leader. I have had this for two weeks already.

Got your eyes open Baby? Guess what? There is nothing I would love better than getting my ever loving hands on you. Boy, are you going to catch the ever loving devil. That is, while we are alone. No Marine is allowed to kiss or hold hands with anybody while in uniform and in public. But Marines are the devil's own while in private, in or out of uniform!

When you write, please use my complete address and do not use anything else on the outside of the letter.

I hope I have enough money to make ends meet. You should be getting something soon from the government. For God's sake Kitten, keep active. The time passes so much faster and is spent so much better.

Lots of love Honey. I think of you constantly. My memories are something I can take out and look at while things are quiet. Believe me they mean a lot. Thanks a lot for those beautiful memories Honey! Boy, I sure hope I have given you the same in return. It really means a lot. Good night beautiful lady. I will write again soon. Be mine Honey, all mine. Good night, Steve. P.S. I love you Honey. Steve.

January 19, 1966: Dearest Husband, Your letters are really great. You sound on top of things, Honey. Keep up the marvelous work! I know you will be one of the best, if not the best.

It will be so great and wonderful to hear your voice! You bet I'll be at your parent's house, on Sunday at 0700!

Darling, I missed you awfully last night. Will I be glad when this is over. You know I keep thinking: Won't it be great when we can start a family. I want to very much. Our little boy or girl; wouldn't that be the greatest ever! You know, I have been thinking about that shower too!

Now for the bad news. The course I signed up for has been cancelled. Not enough people signed up for it, and I am very disappointed.

It must be hard for you not getting any mail for all this time. I really appreciate you writing to me. I think I have a very fine husband.

I bought some varnish remover yesterday while shopping. I plan to start redoing the chair soon. My painting is drying. Maybe I can work on both tonight.

I will go up to your parents with your address! I have spent so much time up there. Your mother is so wonderful, and she wants me to do everything. She thought that I wouldn't have any trouble going to Portland; and that I should, if I wanted to. She encourages me to do new things. So see, nothing happened, and I have returned safely.

While I was in Portland, Sue and I decided that we were glad that we were country girls. We were in the city for a little while, and that we could leave whenever we wanted to, as I did. This is not the place for us to live for a long time.

By the way, this is your test for decoding skills. Reading your wife's writing is a good deciphering exercise anyway. My penmanship could use a lot of improvement.

In the bank today, there was a display of wood products of Carrol County. It was quite good and you would have liked it. I love you my wonderful husband. I am so proud of you! Love, Brent.

January 22, 1966 Quantico, VA: Dear Brent, Good afternoon Kitten. Well, it is Saturday and liberty has been sounded. You have never seen a squad bay empty so fast. No one could or would even think of moving that fast to make a formation, and believe me you move plenty fast for those.

At the moment we have about forty-five candidates in my squad bay. It is hard to tell because of guys going to sick bay and not coming back. Some guys leave for sick bay, and we do not hear or see them again. Others show up after five or six days. After missing seven days a candidate is automatically dropped.

This is like an accelerated course in college. Only difference is that no one is expected to work at his own speed. You are expected to work at a level above what you thought was your capability.

By the way, most of the candidates are coming back! The duty sergeant is sending everyone back to shine their shoes before going on liberty. Everyone has to really shape up to make a go of this program. A Marine just can't be anything except perfect in appearance and bearing.

We are really being put through a good physical conditioning program. The every day program calls for two sessions of physical training. The stress is placed upon developing a strong upper body and coordination. Believe me, when I say that the exercises strain and strengthen every muscle and area in your body. We send a lot of candidates to sick bay every day. And, it seems as if we send the same ones again and again.

Right now it is snowing in sunny Virginia, and I want to tell you that it is really coming down. It is a good thing we do not have anything to do besides take care of our gear this afternoon. I hope it is gone by tomorrow. Wednesday, we have a forced march, and it could be bad in all this snow.

I am certainly glad that you addressed my letter exactly as I gave it to you. It saves the First Sergeant a lot of headaches; and in turn, saves me a little time in the wheelhouse. That is where the wheels (higher ranks) stay—Platoon Commander's Office. You know, you have to show that you can take directions and follow orders, before you can give directions and orders.

Talk about being brain washed: It seems to me that my parents (I never heard your parents voice an opinion.) have brain washed you. You want to start a family, huh. Well, to tell the truth, I would like to do that also.

Can you picture us with our child? Just remember the little monster is all ours. Would not that be something. We had better wait until we get this program behind us. Nothing like being sure we can handle the situation.

I am very glad that you are keeping busy. Keep expanding your interests and skills. I can't tell you how much this really means. Not only to yourself, but to future employers. Be interested in a number of things. I know that this applies to me as well as you. We only go this way once.

Please remember me to your parents and my parents. Tell them I may be able to get a post card off sometime, but that my time is extremely limited. Of course, I could write them by cutting my talk with you short. I think that is a little too drastic.

I have only five uniforms right now. Three are utilities (combat uniforms) and two winter service; tan blouse and green pants. When I graduate, I have to get three different types of just dress uniforms. Right now, I need two more sets of utilities. Wait until you see the uniforms! While I hate to admit it, the uniforms really have me hooked. Every stripe, etc. has its reason or tradition according to the history of the Marine Corps.

As far as the program and how it is run, I will tell you all about it when I see you. That way I can answer questions and keep you from forming false impressions. Do not believe everything you hear from old Marines or otherwise. Your husband can tell you the straight scoop when he sees you. So do not worry about anything. I am here for the sole purpose of becoming a Marine Corps officer. The staff is here to make me one. I am going to become a good one. So do not worry! Everything is alright.

We are not allowed to receive calls here. If a situation arises and the Red Cross is called in; then and only then, will a call go through. In such a case, my address should be enough. The Red Cross would probably get in touch with me. There is no reason in the world why we can't receive letters every day. Do not feel as if you have to write every day; but write often as I want to hear from you. Your letter was wonderful. For fifteen minutes I was back in touch with everyone at home and up to date on all the news. That was a real letter. Still do not send any packages of food. Never during my ten weeks here, do that. That is the only "do not" concerning mail, besides an incomplete address.

This is just like the old Army barracks in "From Here To Eternity." We even have a couple of western boys who know the "Re-enlistment Blues."

I am going to have to close now, Brent. My rifle and boots (a Marine's two first concerns) are awaiting. I can hardly wait until tomorrow morning. You have no idea how much the sound of your voice will mean to me. You great big beautiful girl you. You just wait! This kind of talk is getting me down. You mean so damn much to me. good night Darling, Steve.

January 23, 1966, Moultonborough, NH: Dearest Steve, It was wonderful to hear your voice this morning Honey; even though the connection was not very good. There was not enough time to say everything I would have liked to say. I can hardly wait to see you again.

I think your mother is working on your father for time off in March. It would be nice if they could go to Quantico also. I am looking forward to it ever so much.

It is really storming outside. Another big snowstorm. It is really laying on a lot of snow!

I have spent a lot of time at your parents. I hope they don't get tired of me. Well, I am doing the chair here, my painting has to be done here, so that is why. Furthermore, I truly enjoy being here. Your mother and I just finished combing each other's hair! I styled hers really sexy, and your Dad liked it. There isn't much to do with mine, so I am as usual.

Enclosed is a picture my parent's neighbor took with their new polaroid camera. I am supposed to send it to you, so I did. It was taken near the old tree stump in front of their house. I had been skiing on the hill by the barn so I had my poles, but you can't see the skis!

Missy doggie has recovered nicely from her motherhood state. She is now a frisky little doggie again.

Your mother meant that your letters to me are wonderful. She was concerned that you might think she was being sarcastic, as she was a little upset she hadn't heard personally from you. However, I think she understands your schedule. She wants you to use all your time to really make it good down there. I can't tell you how happy and proud of you all of us are up here. You sound as if you were in your element. You like real challenges, don't you?!

So, I am glad to hear you are going to run a most efficient home, etc. I suppose I am really going to have to shape up. I will not ship out, so shape up it will be!

My parents are fine, I guess. They wonder about my being at your folks so much.

I did a sketch of a girl the other day and surprised myself. It actually looked like a girl.

It was nice to receive a letter from Sue, and she was glad I had visited her. She said hello to you. When Betty wrote, she wanted you to know that she addressed the envelope to Mrs. "Steven" Martin. By the way, why don't you address them as Mrs. "Steven" Martin? I personally like that name!

I am thinking of all the things necessary for the trip to your graduation. Is it the one event or are there other events?

I miss you very much. Your letters are so very sweet. I think that you are thinking up some pretty good ideas too! I have every faith in you Darling. You are the best, most wonderful man in this whole wide world. I am so very, very happy to be your wife.

I hope the Tuesday flight will be wonderful. Good luck sweetheart. I love you so very much. Love, Your wife, Brent (Kitten).

January 23, 1966, Quantico, VA: Dearest Brent, Good evening Honey. I have a little free time (I should admit that I made time.) and I decided to write to my girl.

I can't tell you how wonderful it was to hear your voice today. I had forgotten what a soft, extremely womanly voice you have. Darn you Darling, you just plain turn me on. I miss you something wicked Kitten. I must really love you to miss you this way. I need you Honey: your love, understanding, and your needing me.

Be mine always Kitten, and I truly feel I can take on anything. A woman has to be there for a man; and she must be able to find her strength in knowing that her man honestly loves her, and that he must perform as a man in a sometimes complex society. In other words, the woman remains his anchor while her man does what a man must.

She takes pride in her man for showing that he can be no less than a man, even while inside he wishes he could be with her forever and never parted. I hope you realize this Honey. It is tearing me apart to be away from you; but, I would do the same thing again. I sometimes wish I did not have duties above those of being and satisfying my own wants and needs and those of the person I love. The fact can't be escaped; everybody has duties of greater magnitude that for just himself and his wants. I think you know what I mean.

The reason I am telling you this is that I feel you should know I feel this way about it. You could understand already. I do not want you to feel I never told you. It seemed as if my leaving was a topic we never discussed between just us. I can't stand the thought of you thinking I am not shaken up by our separations; or that it does not hurt me. Well, it does hurt me Kitten. You mean an awful lot to me; I am not ashamed to say I need you desperately. I love you with all my heart and soul.

We have quite a cross section here as far as candidates are concerned. Most of the boys were making all kinds of money on the outside. We have: teachers, engineers, economists. My bunkie was an admissions officer at a major university, and just a few people who are trying to find ways to beat the draft. Boy, did those guys make a mistake coming here. From the frying pan into the fire so to speak.

Tomorrow I have squad leader and the twenty-sixth I pull Corporal-of-the-Guard. From now on in it is every man for himself. Two weeks to learn the ropes and from there on you are on your own.

The youngest candidate is about twenty-one and the oldest is twenty-nine and an ex-Marine. Everyone is just newly graduated from college. A few have one or two years job experience; most just a few months.

Before we make any definite plans about graduation you had better make sure I am going to make it. They will tell us the persons on the last cut about three or four days before the completion of the course. We will make our plans around these requirements. I really do not understand it all, but I honestly feel I will make the grade. Do not kid yourself Honey; this is probably the toughest thing I have ever tried to do. I think, however, I am what they are looking for. I am going to try like hell until they tell me I made the grade, or that it is time to get off.

Continued: January 24,1966, Quantico, VA: Well, Honey, today has finally passed. Tomorrow should be mostly R&R (Rest and Relaxation). A nice plane ride and nothing to do but look around and enjoy the scenery.

Today we had a talk with the Aviation Officer here at Quantico. He said that once we get to the Naval Air Training Station in Florida; we will have two or three moves during the course of our training there. That will give us a chance to see various parts of the Gulf States. Kitten, I have got to make this program. The job I think I will really like, and the advantages to both you and me are well worth the effort.

I was candidate squad leader today. According to the candidate platoon sergeant everyone on duty received an unsatisfactory rating. Do not panic, Darling. The D.I. told the platoon sergeant that a marginal rating is very usual.

The candidate guide received his rating because of scratching his nose in ranks and not coming to the proper position of attention at some time during the day. The Platoon Commander holds office hours Wednesday night. We will, no doubt, find out about it all then.

This morning we took a test on two weeks of material. Military Subjects #1. That's one thing I aced. According to the answers given by the officer in charge, I got a ninety-four. Win some, lose some. Just keep plugging.

We lost two more candidates today. This is the official scoop. They were dropped by an evaluation board because of physical defects. When the fifth week rolls around we expect an even larger number to simply quit. The failure rate is from 20 to 40 percent. At least that is what everyone seems to quote.

Well Honey, I have got to clean my rifle, polish my boots, and shine my brass. Something every Marine does every night. Good night Darling. Give my love to everyone. And, rest assured I would give my right arm to be with you. Good night Kitten, Steve. P.S. Hey girl, I love you!

January 26, 1966, New Hampshire: Dearest Steve. Your letters are wonderful Darling. I love to hear about the things you are doing. I know you will make it, Darling. You have everything it takes. I love you my husband. I miss you more and more every day. I can hardly wait for March 17th to get here. It will be the most wonderful thing in this world to be with you again.

My parents want me to say hello to you. They enjoy your letters too.

Your Dad says your Mother is going to go to your graduation; but she says only if he can go too. So whenever you say, we will "fall in" and come to see you. I am coming no matter whether anyone else can or not! I'll sign and seal this with a kiss. I love you my darling and miss you so very, very much. Love, Your Brent.

January 26, 1966, Quantico, VA: Dear Brent, Good evening Kitten, it is now snowing in sunny Virginia. When I say snowing, I should also say that is has been snowing all day today and looks like it will continue to do so.

Out trip to South Carolina was excellent, but wet. While it was not raining here at Quantico, we really ran into it down south. Needless to say we saw quite a show from a static line of most of the jets, helicopters, and cargo planes used by the Marine Corps, to practical demonstrations of how tactical airfields can be set up anywhere in the world.

At noon we ate in a field mess that even had music playing. I mean to say that the red carpet was really rolled out. I also have the feeling that a lot of dust was swept under the rug, but while they lack some things, they make up for it with good planes and some really fine pilots.

The base was a really good looking place. It was well taken care of and looked a lot better than some posts I have seen. The big sales pitch was made, and they got to a lot of candidates. The two former N.C.O's in my platoon are going to switch over to the aviation program. As they said: "We need pilots!"

We flew down there in three C-130's These three planes picked up all 230 or so of us, with room to spare, and got us there in about one hour and forty-five minutes. These are the big cargo planes with the section that can be dropped down under the tail. They can carry jeeps, small tanks, and one heck of a pile of men. They are also used to refuel other aircraft while in flight.

Well enough of dream land and back to grunt land, as the fly boys call us foot soldiers. Today we had our first forced march. Despite four inches of snow and more snow falling; we fell out complete with rifle, combat pack and utilities. No coats or jackets, just your shirt. Needless to say we did not wait around too long. During the course of our three mile hike, the Captain who commands our platoon fell four times. The last two times he made the candidate platoon guide fall when he did. It pays to keep a straight face when your leaders mess up.

Tonight I got Corporal of the Guard again. I even got the same relief, 2300 to 0100. Next week I have no guard duty, and the only billet I drew was platoon guide. By the way, I was given a marginal as squad leader. While my squad area was not spotless, I had to take over as platoon guide and did a "creditable" job. Therefore I got a marginal. One other billet holder got a marginal, the other two received unsatisfactory. One of these candidates is a former N.C.O. so as you can see you really get picked apart. Trying to get sixteen men to do a job and do it well, while they are worrying about their personal gear, is nearly impossible.

I do not have the full details concerning graduation. To be truthful no one is absolutely sure they will make it. I just know I am going to have one hell of a go at it. Forty-five more minutes and my relief arrives. Then, I will get some shut eye. Honey, will that feel good.

Tomorrow we have bayonet drills for two hours. In the six inches of snow we have now, and with it still coming down, that should be fun.

While at the air station we saw a low-level bomber that the pilot flies entirely by radar. He can't see out towards the bow, even during daylight hours. The darn thing is one huge computer and bomb rack. It can carry half the bomb load of some other planes, but it is flown by only two men, meant to operate close to the deck, and it is blind. Using a teletype system, and where you want to go is placed in a computer. The pilot looking into a screen sees a line representing his flight path. He also sees contours of the terrain around his path of flight. This way he simply flies the plane, using instruments, down the path he sees in the scope. It is designed for use as an all-weather bomber. Periods of stormy or cloudy weather really mean nothing to this bomber.

January 27, 1966: Dear Brent, Well, I am continuing writing on guard again. This time it only amounts to sitting and watching the platoon's rifles and gear. Since yesterday we found out that another candidate has been dropped from our platoon. The guy was having a hard time physically, and he was finally declared not physically qualified.

Bayonet training was not bad at all. We did our dance steps in the classroom, one platoon at a time.

That is a course that should remove any doubt in anyone's mind what Marines are for. Get in and kick the enemy out. Some of the draft duckers are beginning to sweat a little. Quite a few of the Marines we have contact with are being shipped over.

This afternoon we had a lecture from the base duty aviator. The big play was on. They got a good percentage of candidates to make out forms to take the necessary tests for the aviation program. They really act as if they are dying to get pilots. Every time the aviation program is even mentioned, the red carpet comes out.

By the way, a Marine pilot flies every plane he is physically capable of flying. In other words, a hot ticket career officer will fly jets, multi-engine, helicopters, and a desk.

Tonight is haircut night. The Marine Corps says every week, every candidate, shall have his hair cut. That is eighty cents a week that keeps a cool head on your shoulders.

I paid for travel expenses today. Since I am sending some home, do not spend it all in one place. If other needs are not really pressing, I suggest a nice new coat for my one and only!

Well Darling, I must hit the rack. Only ten minutes until lights out. Tonight I got "ready" for an announced inspection tomorrow.

I love you Kitten. I hear that my parents enjoy your presence very much. I enjoy your presence even more, believe you me. Good night beautiful lady. I love you with all my heart and soul. Good night Honey, Steve

January 30, 1966, Wolfeboro, NH: Dearest Steve, What storms! We hear Virginia has her share of snow too.

One month is just about behind us; only one-and- a half months to go! I can hardly wait as I miss you so much, and it seems so long.

Well, I finally did it. My mother and I went shopping. I bought a coat, and I hope you will like it.

My allotment still hasn't come. Guess I'll have to put most of it away as I have done my big spending for now. Although, I wonder if I'll be able to save enough to fly down to see you. It would cost about $52.00 to fly round trip Boston to Washington, D.C.

Right now my parents are looking at our wedding pictures. I like to look at them also, especially the one with you and Auntie. You look so very handsome, and I love you my great big hunk of a man!

I have finally finished reading the book "Exodus" and it was a great story. Have started reading "From The Terrace" now.

When you graduate, and we come down, will you and I be able to stay together? Wait until I get my hands on you, Sir. Just you wait! My diamond is sparkling; are you thinking of me, maybe?

I sure do miss you and wish you were here. I want you home so very much. I love you! Brent.

January 30, 1966, Quantico, VA: Dearest Brent, good afternoon Honey. We are having a New England afternoon here in Virginia. Last night we got another six inches of snow. Believe me, they do not know what to do with a foot or so of snow. Traffic is completely tied up for miles around. The candidates who went to Washington and made it back, say the city is pretty much tied up in knots. Cars are stuck all along the freeways, and there was even a snow plow stuck out in front of the barracks. Boy, do the really lack the proper equipment for handling snow.

Boy, I could stand seeing you right now. I do not know how I am going to stand not seeing and holding you Darling. It seems like years ago since I last saw you. What I would not give to have you in my arms again. There would be no getting away once I got my hands on you. I want you to wear a lot of nice pants and sweaters when I come home. I keep remembering what a stunningly beautiful woman you are. I love you Darling, and I need you something wicked. I need you physically. Honey, do you remember how often we use to make love to each other? Be my girl, darling. Save yourself for me. Lots of love, Steve.

January 31, 1966, Quantico, VA: Dearest Brent. Good evening darling. I hope you are busy making all sorts of improvements to your painting and the job you did to our first real antique. You can bet I am really looking forward to seeing all of these things.

We have one candidate still out from leave. Three from our platoon were listed as "over-the-hill." Two have come in since the list was published. That could be enough to ruin their chances of making it for these candidates.

We have been shoveling snow with our entrenching tools; and Sunday night we broke out the school streets by marching, in company mass, up and down the streets. Boy, is that lots of fun. They have also cut our mess to two meals as long as we do not have school.

The entire area is pretty well tied up. Nothing moved for a day in this area. There was a report of about a thousand cars being left on one of the routes entering Washington, D.C. You really can't picture this in your wildest dreams. Everything just shut down; no buses, no taxis, and almost no train service. Just like Alaska, except here, they do not have sled dog teams when they need them.

Tomorrow we have a weapons exam, and I hold the billet of platoon guide. I hope everything runs smoothly and that I manage a good score on that exam. Honey, I love you very much. I hope you will find the capacity to love me when this program finally spits me out as a bright new, highly polished, Marine Second Lieutenant. You can't help but go through a change in your outward appearance and the way you react to situations. If I do make the grade, I could seem different in some ways; but believe me, you have to put on a certain expected face to get a particular job done. In other words, I might growl and yell more when I get out of here; but I am still the same guy. Actually, I think the training will prove very effective; just what I really needed.

I am really looking forward to seeing you Brent. I am going to be shining that beautiful day, you can bet. Say, do not forget to wear a nice pair of tight pants. Girl, I spend a good deal of my time just dreaming about that beautiful figure of yours displayed in form fitting clothes. Hey, do not look at me that way! Remember, I am married to you, it is legal now! Love, Steve.

February 1, 1966, Quantico, VA: Good evening Honey. Well the training day is ended, and the liberty call has been sounded. My billet did not go the best, nor did the weapons exam. But as in everything here, I have learned a number of valuable lessons. I have to be more forceful, in the sense that when I have a billet, it has to be my way or my neck.

The test was really one in a sort of gray zone. You know, the real tricky kind. I could get a grade of either an eighty-eight or ninety. I think it was the highest, but everyone's average dropped on this one.

While I was platoon guide they switched part of the physical training. Up until now the guide only let the platoon in what is known as the daily seven. Today they wanted us to lead rifle exercise also. I did alright, except that I did not know beyond three drills; he wanted four different drills, naturally.

It is snowing out again. The forecast is for around four inches. Brother, this really should be interesting to see if they have learned anything from last weekend. It should be interesting to see if they can handle this amount. Down here they wait until the snow storm is all over; then they start plowing. Not like at home when the roads are pretty much kept open during a storm.

Tomorrow we have a conditioning march of three hours in length. Friday we have another of three miles that is a speed march. The last march we had, if you remember, was really slippery. One of the warrant officer candidate companies lost two men with broken legs on the same trail, after we got the trail broken out.

By God Kitten, you know what, your Marine husband is going to the OC Club and buy a hamburger and a beer. By God, it is time I took some time off. I am going to spend some of our precious money on a purely selfish thing. Food!

It is the end of the month and mess is really slender. This morning there were only two pancakes and three pieces of toast; when you are used to four eggs and piece of meat alongside of those two pancakes and pieces of toast! Boy, we are on a diet!

I have got to close now, Darling. I love you Kitten. See you soon, Steve.

February 3, 1966, Moultonborough, NH: Dearest Steve, Only "NEXT" month and I will see you my husband. We do have a lot of snow up here too. You should be right at home down there, after all!

Missy doggie is looking at me as though she wants to say something. She says "hello" to you and that she is gaining weight and looks good again.

We will have to discuss our expenses and allotments soon. I started this letter with the intention of not having you worry about finances now. I doubt that I have accomplished this. We have time to discuss it later.

I miss you very much sweetheart, and I would like to see you. I hope things are going well for you. I know you are working very hard.

Your parents are very happy with receiving your letter. I also enjoyed it. Your dad has a bad back, but I do not know why. He was reading "The Green Berets" tonight, as I had it, and forgot about it until I heard the song again. There is now a song about then if you haven't heard.

I'm glad you remember all the things we shared, Steve. If possible, it will be even better when we are together again. You miss what you have the most, when it is gone. Just think, a second honeymoon already! I love you very much. You are my everything. Please return safely.

My parents send their best wishes to you also. Goodnight my love. Love, Brent.

February 3, 1966, Quantico, VA: Dearest Brent, Good afternoon Darling. Today has not gone half bad at all, so far. We have had bayonet training (I won all six of my matches.) and individual movement under fire. This last particular part of our training had such nice things as low and high crawl, the rush, and the hands and knees movement. Picture for yourself on an unbroken field of snow a foot and a half deep. We low and high crawled, rushed, and reacted to overhead flares and ground flares. One hundred yards out, turn around and back. Talk about wet, boy, we were soaked. Our rifles were just plane stuffed with snow; everything was full of snow. Now comes the topper: we had one hell of a good time!

With all the shouting and yelling you would have thought that the Rebels were at it again. Real "gung ho" you know. We made the other platoons sound sick. The last forced march we had we only had seven candidates fall behind. Our file leaders were bodily throwing members of other platoons off the road into the snow banks. We ate up a good half of the platoon ahead of us. Gained a lot of friends that day.

I hope your new coat has pleased you. If the style and color meet your standards, I am quite sure I will like it very much. Of course, there is a little bias there; I am in love with the model.

From my very active spy network operating in your area, I hear that your painting is very presentable. Keep up the good work, and remember, no person with true artistic taste ever creates something he truly feels is perfection that can't be improved. Just keep at it. It will help you see a side of the world and life that would have been hidden behind a closed door, otherwise.

There are so many closed doors in life just waiting for someone to crack them open to pass beyond. How many people just open one door or two, and leave themselves with just those four walls to look at. Good God Honey, we owe our parents more than just that. We also owe someone a great deal bigger than ourselves something for the brains and abilities we were born with. In a few words, keep looking for new horizons to explore and develop.

Boy, I had better get down off my soap box, huh! I am very glad you have started doing a little more reading. It helps pass the winter nights and helps enlarge the mind. Sounds good, huh? But it is the truth, and all one really needs to do is form the habit. Less spare time and more results from your spare time, or what would have been your spare time. There are so many opportunities just for the taking. In your field and in any other field you are interested in or think you might enjoy.

You actually dare mention the Army to me Girl? You will give fifty-five "Semper Fidelis" in a nice loud voice to pay for that mistake. "Green Berets," my foot! They are nothing compared with Force Recon. These guys chew up Special Forces men for practice. They land ahead of the regular forces and cut off re-enforcements. They skin dive, parachute, and sign up for five and a half years of service after completing basic training. Our company executive officer is one of these guys. They are tough beyond belief.

I have got to clean my rifle, Honey. Believe me, I wish I was playing games with you. Until I write again Honey, good night. I love you Darling. Lots of love, Steve.

February 5, 1966, Quantico, VA: Dearest Brent, Good afternoon Darling. The weather is warmer and the snow is starting to settle here.

Something like spring at home, but I have a feeling that spring will be short lived here.

Everyone is talking about the evaluation board that is due to meet next week. Word has it that two candidates from our platoon will be called before it. If they are dropped, that will cut our platoon from the original forty-nine to an even forty. Our platoon has lost more candidates than any other platoon. All other platoons have lost only three candidates each. We have lost more than twice that number.

Our duty instructor came by and visited us last night. He checked all the wall and foot lockers to see if they were locked. He found three wall lockers unlocked and took the weapons from them. In the entire company he got twelve rifles.

As I have told you there are certain things that a Marine never does; one of these is mistreat his rifle. If a Marine drops his rifle, he has to maintain constant contact with it for twenty-four hours. This give you an idea of what happens to Marines who allow their weapons to be stolen. They had better have a lot of fun on this liberty, because they are going to get it.

Tomorrow we have a test on Marine Corps history. I have got to get busy so that my average will stay up there where it belongs. Since my leave, or rather my amount of leave has a direct bearing on my standing, I want to do an excellent job.

I am getting so that I am spending more and more time at the Candidates Club. Last night I took a half hour off and went over and had a couple of beers with my bunkie. I like to listen to the music. I am going to see that we have a stereo. I really miss the noise you know I like so well.

Well Honey, I have got to go over that history so I am going to have to close. I miss you Darling. I am really looking forward to seeing you again. Keep yourself busy, Honey. The remaining time will fly by. Work on your painting as I am really looking forward to seeing the results of your effort. I hope you can see a lot of results for the work I have put in here for the last ten weeks.

I guess you and I will have to go on a sightseeing tour. If things continue this way, I will not see anything around here before we do it together. Until I write again, Kitten. I love you very much. Say hi to everyone. Lots of love, Steve.

February 8, 1966, Quantico, VA: Dearest Brent., Good evening Honey. I hope today was a good one for you. Everything is just fine here in Grunt Land. Today it was a twenty foot rope climb, mountain clime, and a three mile run; all with rifle, hard hat, and combat pack. It feels wonderful to be sitting here right now. My average was somewhere in the nineties. On the run I came in fifth, not so very good. If I had really put out, I should have finished first. This is not place for "all-so-rans!"

Our home of record, as far as the service is concerned, is Wolfeboro, NH as that was where we lived when I enlisted. I think it would be a good idea to operate as if Moultonborough, NH was our home of record. I am much more familiar with the town structure there. Besides, that is where my parents are and they can give you help with things.

Hey Darling, I am in love with you. I am also tired. If we were together, would you stop working long enough to hold my head in your lap? That would be unbelievable. I would easily take at least one hundred years of that kind of care. Believe it or not we look forward to our weekly haircuts because of the one minute of personal attention we get.

I think you and I are going to cause family trouble by seeing lots of you and me alone. I have thought of a lot of things to talk to you about, Kitten.

I hear that Congress has passed another G.I. Bill. That gives us some more college, Brent. Just have to get more learning for the both of us, Honey. A Master's degree would mean a lot to me, and you could pick up some of the more specialized phases of your profession. Darn it, we go this way just once.

The Commanding Officer of the Officer Candidate Schools inspected us this morning. One streak of ribbons and brass and a hundred mistakes later, it was all over. He did not take my rifle, or ask me any questions. He just looked me over, grabbed a magazine from my belt, looked at it, and returned it. I think he wanted to see if I would drop my rifle when I saw his right hand move.

I do not know why he did not do something with me. Maybe he thought I was beyond saving. Anyway, he is a Colonel, and I am only a private first class. I guess I do not have to understand.

What the hell are you reading "Green Berets" for? You should be remembering what service your husband is in. For God's sake read "Battle Cry." Now that is a story. In all seriousness, I am very glad to hear that you are reading more now. It is really worthwhile.

I miss you Kitten. I would like to get nice and close to you and go to sleep. Boy, that would be heaven. Just you and me and a lot of time to do whatever we want to. I have got to do my boots, rifle, and brass. I will write again soon. Keep busy. Love, Steve.

February 9, 1966, Moultonborough, NH: Dearest Steve, Everyone was very pleased to receive your letters. They are so very interesting.

I hope you are developing a good "lap" along with your physical exercises. I intend to do a lot of sitting on it when you get home. So you better start shaping it up for many hours of sitting.

What? Are they putting you on a diet; only two meals a day! I can imagine I will have quite a time with you when you get home. I'll have to have a big breakfast ready and waiting. Guess I'll have to shape up!

I am glad the time is passing quickly for you. It does pass much faster when you are busy. It seems to go faster for me when I am at your parents. I have been with your parents so much. I wish I didn't get so down when I am at my parents. I feel closer to you up there with yours.

I shall close for now to go mail this. I hope you have a nice Valentine's Day. March, march, march! I love you my great big Valentine. Only one more month. Just you wait! Love, Brent.

February 11, 1966, Center Tuftonboro: Dearest Steve, You really like to make a person feel guilty, don't you! Have you ever done a good job of writing!

I am glad to hear there is a little money in the air around here. I guess we will just about make ends meet.

So, why can't I read "The Green Berets?" You did, and you seemed to like it. (Of course, I know you were teasing me.) You can't have all work down there and no play.

I am really looking forward to our time together, and I hope we can have some sightseeing also. You are about the greatest sight I want to see right now though.

I was wondering if I could get that dependent's ID card up here. I shall see. By the way, I'm not 5 feet, 9 inches tall, and I only weigh 146 lbs. and not 160 lbs. Good grief. Are you sure you are thinking of the right girl? Only kidding. Also, I am only 5 feet, 8 inches tall!

How would you like to see me in a black lace dress? That is what I might get for an evening dress: black lace.

Today the temperature is up to 53 degrees. Quite a change from 15 degrees below. The yard is now covered with ice.

I suppose I should warn you that I'm going to test your defensive skills; because, I am going to a-t-t-a-c-k you! I plan to use all of the guile known to womankind and really get to you. Just you wait! You think the Marines are tough? Wait until you meet Mrs. Martin again!

My mother and I went into the bank yesterday, and they had a painting of my parent's farm on display. That was a surprise. I am including a picture of the wood products display that I told you about before. Thought you might be interested.

Well, goodnight for now Darling. Only five more weeks! I miss you very much and can't wait to see you. Take really good care of yourself. Love, Brent.

February 11, 1966, Quantico, VA: Dearest Brent, Good afternoon Honey. I hope this letter finds you hard at work on your painting. Everything is fine here; but, I still have got to push harder. You do not make a good Marine in only five short weeks. Our platoon staff is really squared away; if anyone can help me, it is them.

This morning we had an inspection by the company commanding officer. Once again he went through here like a whirlwind. After he was done, the platoon commander and sergeant instructor came right back through the remains. Some days it does not pay to get out of the rack. So far this week, we have had bayonet training (I took my six bouts again.) and a conditioning hike. I was "lucky" as I was chosen to be a stretcher bearer. That means you run most of the way at the rear of the column. What makes it interesting is that you carry all the normal gear plus a stretcher for every two men. The other man carries the two rifles.

We had one candidate lose consciousness during the hike. One other candidate, myself, and two sergeants had to carry him out to where the trucks could get in. That was one mile of up-hill trotting that I thought would never end. One other candidate had an attack of heat exhaustion; but, he did not pass out. He simply kept marching not paying any attention to things around him.

In all fairness, I must say it was the best hike we have had, that is, the easiest. It all really amounts to your mental condition. They give up like there is no tomorrow. We had twenty-four drop out of my platoon, but I ran one hell of a lot further and fortunately felt fine.

Enough of this gung-ho junk. I am not writing you to brag because I darn well do not have any reason to brag. Until you are giving your all, you are not really giving yourself in a degree near the dedication you should have.

I have looked high and low and I just can't find a Valentine. Marines do not give their girls lacy hearts with sweet endearments written on them. Just the same I would like to get one for my girl.

Is my love pure? Just look at that heart, white as the driven snow! (A heart was drawn on the white page.) Lots of love Kitten. Please always be my Valentine! Steve. So there you are Honey, with lots of love from your "tough" Marine.

Well Darling, we are very near the halfway mark. Just a little while longer and we will be together again. This weekend is the halfway point. Now is the time to really turn on the steam.

My bunkie just passed the Naval Flight Officer physical. Those are the boys who ride in the back seat and drop the ordinance. Who knows, someday he and I may work one of those big jets together. I would not mind it at all, he will be good at it. What I really want is a "Skyhawk." It is a sweet little jet that is used for ground support. The only problem is that a man has to be very compact to fit into the darn thing!

Hey girl, I love you. I love you very much. Do not let this gung-ho business bother you. I have got to dedicate myself to the job of getting my bars, then my wings. One thing this program has given me is the determination that I will never be beaten, never worked into the ground; I will be at the front of my unit. Hard work can put me there.

To say the least Darling, I miss you very much. That could have given me some of this feeling. I just have to bring those bars home to you. More important is the advancement it will mean in our lives.

This weekend my bunkie and I plan to sleep, clean and polish boots, and study drill. Now tell me that I would not rather hold, polish, and study my lovely wife. You can bet your life, and quite safely, that I would give anything to be with you. If you came down now, I think having to say good-bye to you again would really be too hard.

Besides, for two weeks before and two weeks after that fateful weekend, I would be absolutely no good. Needless to say I would really like to see you, but I am holding out for a few days of sightseeing around and about historic Virginia when you do get here. Washington must also offer more than bars and "Go-Go" joints. I think the primary concern of my sightseeing will simply consist of looking at my beautiful wife. Now that is a sightseeing view worth viewing. Girl, I just plain love you, in fact, I am crazy about you. Just think of all the wonderful memories we share. We really had a great big taste of what heaven must be like. I think you and I must have what it takes to have a happy marriage and a wonderful life together. Lady, I really miss you. I want you so dam bad Kitten. It seems like forever since I last held you; by the way you fit there, just like you were made to order for my arms. I like that idea very much, it means a lot to me. Keep busy and show everyone what you and our marriage are made of. Good night Darling, Steve.

(Brent was not sure how to address the vein of thought found in some of the letters from Steve, written during their first separation and those horrible months while he was in Vietnam. In reading passages again from his letters, it was indicated that he was hearing from his fellow servicemen about marital fidelity; or lack of it in their lives. It was if they questioned Steve's beliefs regarding his relationship with his wife. Maybe the concept of love and fidelity was foreign to them; but it was one that Steve and Brent shared unequivocally. Yes, it was the 60's—free love, etc. However, Steve and Brent had found what they needed, in each other.)

February 13, 1966, Center Tuftonboro, NH: Dearest Steve. Don't look out the window! It is snowing again! A lot of previous snow has melted in the last few days anyway, so there will not be as much accumulation.

Last night my father used our car. When he came back in the house he said: "I'm not sure I have that car in park very well." I had a funny feeling, so I said: "You better check it again." On second thought, I said: "I'll go do it." Just as I opened the front door, I head the wheels start to roll! It was half way across the yard when I got to it and stopped it. Boy, I shook for half an hour! It was headed towards the snow bank, so it probably wouldn't have done any harm. Still, I didn't like having that happen.

There, how was that for a bit of excitement? I have had dreams of chasing wild cars—have you? I remember my father's horse truck used to do that once and awhile. The horses were in it too!

Hi Honey, thanks so much for calling! I only wish I could have heard you better. I hardly know I've talked with you. I thought at first it was my brother. So, it was sure nice to have it be you!

The places we will live seem unbelievable. How am I supposed to get work? Part time baby sitter? Well, if I have a prosperous husband I suppose I won't have to worry. May I work for you? I'll do anything—even sit on your lap.

Thank you so much for the Valentine. It was better than any bought one! My real tough Marine is an artist!

I must close now, Darling. See you soon. Now we are half way there! You bet your life I'll be in Virginia to see you next month. I'll beg, buy or "steal?" my way there. (Preferably the second one!) I love you, my husband! Love, Brent.

February 14, 1966, Quantico, VA: Dearest Kitten, Good evening Honey. A happy Valentine's Day. That is, if you will be my Valentine.

Today, we lost a candidate from the program. That leaves us with forty-one candidates and six of these were called before the evaluation board. I think most of these will be able to continue; but, they have told these persons they had better get on the ball.

Enough of this stuff. More of what Valentine's day is for. Did I ever enjoy listening to you talk. You sound so damn sexy, Lady. A nice soft voice that is just a little throaty. Brother, do you ever sound beautiful and like you are a regular devil, you know where.

Well, now you know the truth is finally out. I think you are a beautiful woman who enjoys being just that. Honey, I want to break the news to you slowly, but Marines never go on the defensive; they think only of the attack! But, I must admit that this is one battle I am going to really enjoy.

When I graduate from flight training, I get civilian licenses for all the planes I have trained in. The other interesting fact, and the reason we are getting such a big push towards aviation is the airlines hire the service pilots as soon as their service hitches are completed. The money these pilots get paid is really unbelievable. It will give us something to think about in any case.

I am going to be very happy to see you. You probably will not want to be seen with me because of my hair cut. If you pull that on me, I am going to be really mad.

I do agree the other services have their place. The Navy, for example is needed to transport the Marine Corp from shore to shore. As you can see, I am completely objective and not at all biased. I want you to feel this way also; but then, such things require lots of personal instruction. May I offer my services?

Boy, I want you to know that Washington gets to be a more "swinging" place every weekend. I guess the guys are slowly finding out the more serious "fun" spots. Some of the tales they bring back. I am glad I have a woman of your beauty and caliber Brent. I really mean this from the bottom of my heart.

A lot of the guys can't understand me staying here weekends and not "living(?)" it up, simply because I am married. Moreover, they do not understand that I really do not worry about you being alone for a while; aside of worry about your health, money situation, etc. They just do not believe in our brand of love. I feel sorry for those people who can't trust enough to really love. I really love you just as I know you really love me. I know our faith in each other is well founded. Good night Darling, Steve.

February 16, 1966, Quantico, VA: Dearest Brent, Good evening, Honey. Well, it is a rainy day here in Virginia, Darling. The rain and clouds made them cancel our tactical helicopter hop today. You know, they get us aboard and then set us down behind "enemy" lines.

Since we just got back from a night compass hike and camping out, the effect of speed and ease would have been firmly imprinted on our minds. As you can see, they are always thinking.

We had a total of eight candidates go before the evaluation board today. One candidate is leaving for parts unknown. The others were told that they were failing thus far, and the remaining three and a half weeks had better show some improvement.

Boy, the first part of this week has simply flown by. They have kept us really busy and always on the move, and this helps to no end.

The twentieth of this month is creeping right up. I have no idea what my pay will be. Just take a guess!

Say hello to your parents for me. I am afraid that I forgot all about anything or anyone else but you last Sunday. I really did not mean to be in the least rude, but I did manage anyway.

I enjoy your letters very much. They add a very bright spot to my day. I really like to hear about things at home and what everyone is doing.

What did you mean in your letter about you getting a job? We will be moving to different bases the first year or so, and you don't have to worry about working. They do pay me for all this fun I am having.

Well, I have to get busy as a lot of things need doing. I love you Brent S. Martin. I will be seeing you soon. Take care. I will write tomorrow. I have guard duty now. Good night Baby, Steve.

February 17, 1966, Quantico, VA: Dearest Brent, Well Kitten, tonight I have Corporal of the Guard again. This time, at least, they gave me a different shift. It affords me the opportunity to write to you.

As you realize, we are a rather select group of young men, and the one thing we all have in common is that we are aggressive, and growing more so every day. That combined with the fact that we are under a lot of stress, gives rise to a particular type of individual.

So, I am disappointed in some people's feelings towards service in the armed forces. We all owe so very much to our country; and there is no rule that says everyone must serve in the same way. You have to go ahead and study the entire setup to get the most out of it; but, a lot of guys are afraid to even look at any part of the armed services. There are jobs teaching children of servicemen, and that way get to see other countries. The chances are honestly unlimited.

One of the guys here is having a problem with a friend. He has told people not to send any cards or packages of food. What arrives but a big 24" X 24" card on Valentine's Day, and a huge package of cookies; not to mention a big red heart on the outside of the box. You think the platoon staff is not having fun with him. He is about to wring someone's neck. We are anxiously awaiting the next development. I will keep you informed!

Today we had a conditioning hike. One of our D.I.'s (Drill Instructors) set out to run us into the ground. He ended up straggling in after our platoon. We ran him into the ground. We are getting into good shape, and you do not get people to quit like you did the first few hikes.

Well Kitten, Only twenty-eight more days. The actual program will last only three more weeks. The last week is strictly practice for graduation and various administrative tasks. I do believe I will put my head in your lap and sleep a year. I am in a constant state of numbness. Just the same, I find myself able to accomplish more and more each passing day. It is a good feeling to go through a program like this. You learn a lot about your strong and weak points.

I am really all fired up to get started on this grand life of ours together. I honestly feel we will make the grade in a big way. More learning on formal and informal grounds will be one of our hallmarks. Everyone needs a lot of both.

This is the amazing thing about this program. Most guys here have very little practical knowledge of almost anything. Most of them have a lot of money, either backing them or in their own right. When I look around, I see my parents did a terrific job of preparing me to be on my own. A lot of these guys just lack any knowledge of how to do for themselves. Tonight, I had to reassemble a rifle for a candidate. He has had the rifle for six weeks, and he still can't rapidly field strip it.

133

Speaking about stripping, how are you Sexy? I would like to have my hands on you right now. That my dear girl, is heaven! It is going to be so good to see you again. I can hardly wait. Kitten. You mean so darn much to me.

I hope you had a chance to visit your brother. I bet his kids have changed almost completely. Well Kitten, the end of my watch has arrived, back to bed. I love you Baby. Goodnight Kitten, Steve.

February 17, 1966, Center Tuftonboro, NH: Dearest Steve. Only one more month Darling! Gosh, I am proud of you!

Did you know that, at present, your father is planning to drive to Virginia? Won't that be nice! I should be busy the next month just getting things done. That will make the time go faster. We will talk about finances later.

I was ambitious yesterday, but I feel lazy today. The flu is going around and I hope my cold goes no further. Our dog, Missey is ambitiously wagging her tail to say hello to you. She wants a hug from you as much as I want a kiss-hug from you. Do you think you could humor us?

Good night for now Honey. I love you so very much. Love, Brent.

February 22, 1966, Center Tuftonboro, NH: Dearest Steve, Tonight your mother really has the "cold" that has been going around. We both thought we were over it, and then it came back.

Your dad picked up a new battery for us today. The other day I bought some jumper cables to use if we need to jump start it. Everything just to keep the car on the road! Your Dad suggests waiting to register our car later.

Thursday, my parents and I will go to the Court House in Ossipee to finish up details about my grandparent's estate. I thought it was done, but apparently not. Monday or Tuesday I will go to Manchester to get my military identification card. That is where the recruiter told me to go. Your mother would like to shop there also.

It was so nice to hear your voice again. It won't be long now before I see you! Hey, I love you. You better plan on appeasing a well-rested, lonely wife of yours. Good night for now Darling. Continue to do a good job. Take care of yourself. Love, Brent.

February 22, 1966, Quantico, VA: Dearest Brent, Good evening Honey. Do I ever miss you little girl! The days seem to be going slower and slower, and I miss you more with each passing moment. These last three weeks loom as large as centuries right now. I just can't help missing you as if it were my right arm; instead of my wife. You have become too much a part of me.

Am I ever going to be glad to see you. I have been away seven weeks too long, there can be no doubt concerning that. These days off give me too much time to think and remember. I have a lot to recall too. We have some beautiful memories, Darling.

Enough of my feeling sorry for myself. I am very lucky to have those memories and such a bright future. In the long run, we will do better if I get my bars. Then, my wife can be with me most of the time; and we will be able to see a little more of our country and maybe the world.

I hope you realize how much hearing your voice means to me. I know I don't have anything really important to say; but, I just have to hear your voice. God, is it nice to hear your woman's soft, low voice.

Today and tomorrow I have the billet of Candidate Platoon Sergeant. Tomorrow we have a conditioning hike, so I should have a chance to really prove myself. I have got to keep to keep pushing and constantly trying to get a higher rating. A lot of hard work, but exceedingly well worth it. We lost another candidate yesterday. That leaves us with thirty-nine candidates out of our original fifty.

By the way, word has it that a candidate's wife or mother can pin his bars on. As you can see, I really need you down here for graduation. Besides, a number of the guys want to meet my dark eyed Greek. They have already got the word: you can look, but don't touch!

Well Kitten, I have got to get busy getting the various clean-ups organized. I have got to do well on this billet. So far my billets have been about average, actually a little above average.

That is taken care of. Use your squad leaders I always say. Besides, squad leaders are always so eager to do all kinds of work.

Until I can write again, this is your love sick Marine bidding you a fond goodnight! Lots of love Baby! Goodnight Darling, Steve.

February 24, 1966, Quantico, VA: Dearest Brent. Good afternoon Baby. Well it has been a long, long day. We spent the entire day in the field working on squad tactics. It snowed, rained, and I was darn wet all day. We lost five candidates out of our platoon on the hike out. Another day in the glorious history of the Marine Corps.

My tour of duty as Candidate Platoon Sergeant ended 1645 yesterday. We had a conditioning hike that afternoon, so we had an excellent chance to do well. I got a satisfactory rating as Platoon Sergeant, one of about only six or seven that have been given out. My squad leaders all got the satisfactory ratings. This is the first time that this has ever happened.

I had five candidates straggle out of the platoon. Three of these gave up on the very last hill. I screamed and yelled and those guys just stopped. It makes you mad when you have kicked and carried them for the last five miles. The platoon commander marked me satisfactory in endurance, bearing, knowledge, and a few other areas. I would rather have had those guys end the hike where they started.

Enough of this stuff. While it may be important, it is hard for people outside the system to understand. You will become a part of the Corps soon enough. I do not plan on letting you be anything but proud of the Marine Corps. Believe me, it is the only service of its kind.

I can't tell you how much I am looking forward to having a great big steak dinner and dancing with you. None of this wild stuff, just nice and slow, something you can dance to. That means you will have to waltz with me Kitten. No way around it, short of going home to mother! I really hope we get a chance to spend a few relaxed evenings together. I have some wonderful plans and ideas. I am sure you do also. It will be interesting to see what happens when we get together again.

Your letters are wonderful Kitten. I enjoy hearing about home and what my busy wife is up to. A black lace dress sounds very classy. You are not planning to give me any chance at all. Just remember, in the end, it is you who does not stand a chance to escape!

The "word" has it that the Aviation Officer Candidates may only get traveling time to Florida. So dear Lady, look for suitable clothes for Florida! They say the weather is just fine in Florida, and I hope there will be time to sit on the beach.

I am telling you Kitten we have got a few close to the vest months ahead of us. We have our present debts, which we can close out fairly rapidly, and on top of these we have my uniform bills. I think we can do it alright, but we must be careful about where we spend our coins. You willing to try Kitten? By God Darling, we will have a go at it and see how much dust we can stir up. Well, to cleaning my rifle and fixing up my pack. I am looking forward to seeing you. I miss you Honey. Goodnight Darling, Steve.

February 28, 1966, Center Tuftonboro, NH: Dearest Steve, Hello Honey. How are you Mr. Wonderful? Your handsome self, I hope.

I am in a rare mood tonight. "We," our two mothers, the girls, and I went to Manchester today to get my I.D. card. What a circus. We had a good time though. I drove a family car as ours wouldn't start, per usual.

One of the people on the checklist in Tuftonboro is finding out which town I can legally register to vote in now. That shall be interesting.

Only three more weeks Steve! You can't imagine how much I want to see you. I was sad you didn't call last night. I thought maybe you would, but maybe you will next Sunday. How is everything going Darling? I love you so much. Please come home to me soon.

Your parents and I went out to the Laconia Country Club to see the sled dog racers go by. It was fun and a doctor won the race.

Just you wait. You are going to get more love than you ever thought possible. So there. Take that and that! Wait until I get my hands on you! Watch out! I'm warning you right now. Prepare to do battle. Love Brent.

February 28, 1966, Quantico, VA: Dear Brent, Good afternoon Honey. Boy, is it ever raining here in Quantico. Somehow, rain and field problems always seen to arrive at the same time. Needless to say, I am wet and not in the very best of moods at this very moment.

Well, it is another glorious day in the history of the Marine Corps. Today we got some of the cover information. One of the Aviation Officer Candidates was told by a certain aviation officer that many of us might not receive our orders until about two weeks after graduation. So there appears to be a chance of me being stationed here at Quantico for a while. I think I would rather go directly to flight training.

This last weekend I went off the Officer Candidate School section of the base for the first time. I managed to get my pay check cashed and took in a movie. I should never have paid my fifteen cents to get in. It was "Strange Bed Fellows" with Rock Hudson and Gina L. Darn it, she reminded me so much of you. One seduction (All nice and legal husband and wife, they had been separated.) scene was enough to start me walking towards home and you.

Boy, does she remind me of you! The tan skin, real dark hair, and those flashing eyes. Of course, there were other points that also brought you to mind; but just what they are, I will whisper in your ear sometime soon.

Hey Kitten, not much more time left is there. In a short while you will be heading south. I think you will find that our northern section of the country is really outstanding in terms of scenic value, climate, and the standard of living. I have never seen so many small, run down houses in all my life as there are here.

I have not made it to Washington, so that is one thing you and I can experience together. I am personally looking forward to a relaxed meal in a nice quiet steak house. Oh boy, to eat a good meal in peace and quiet. No more sergeants with voices like "Thor" himself.

Tonight looks like a big cleaning day. Rifles, boots, brass, and laundry has to be done. I am just tired thinking about it.

We are down to thirty-nine candidates now. I am afraid another five candidates will be dropped as unsatisfactory at the final board. One of these candidates is a really good guy.

For your information the base operated stores offer goods at below normal cost to servicemen and their dependents. Some small savings, but they add up.

Time for chow. See you soon. Lots of love, Darling. Good night honey, Steve.

March 1, 1966 Quantico, VA: Dearest Brent, Today we have field problems all day. It looks like an interesting day. I am glad to get it all out of the way. Each day gone I am closer to my commission and my wife.

Everyone is spending all kinds of money right now. Uniforms, swords, and accessories are going like hotcakes. My bunkie spent five hundred dollars last night. Your husband plans on spending at least that much sometime soon. Can you imagine the fuss I would make if you spent that sum on dresses. Now, don't get any ideas! I have to have all of this stuff. I have no choice.

You should see me now Kitten. I bet you will see a lot of changes. (For the better I hope!) I know you will have changed. My suit coat size has increased to forty-one long as compared to the forty I took when I started. As you see, I am growing fat and lazy here at Quantico. I definitely need more running. I realize this is a lot to ask, but could you help me on this? What I think is needed is something for me to run after. Of course, the goal must be something really worth the trouble. Now you are what I consider definitely a worthwhile goal. (In all seriousness you do not have to worry about me getting either fat or lazy while I am here!)

Hey Kitten, you know I would like a date with you to walk on the beach at Panama City. A nice moonlit night and my favorite girl. What else could a guy want? Maybe a good steak or seafood dinner under his belt, but nothing else I am sure.

Dam it Kitten, it seems like years ago when I last saw you. Our separation is starting to prey more and more upon my mind. It has gotten so that I look forward to your letters and talking to you on the phone to such a degree that this is all I think about. This is not the best of situations for a person in my position; but, I am not going to stop loving and missing my wife. I guess I will just have to wait for these eighteen days to pass, as they surely must.

That is one big consideration whenever I think about making the service a career. During my hitch, I would no doubt be separated from you for some fairly long periods of time. This situation would get bigger the higher my rank. There still would be quite long separations. I do not really dig this idea at all. I guess we will have to wait before making a decision on that subject. Good morning Darling. I miss you. See you soon. Love, Steve.

March 2, 1966, Tuftonboro, NH: Dearest, Darling Steve. Happy fifth month anniversary! Only 17 more days! Oh boy, oh boy! I don't know what to do first.

Right now I am at my parents waiting for my brother to get here this evening. They will be here until Friday. Last night I went over to the Laconia Nursing School to see my old classmates. They were glad to see me, as I them. Everyone was flashing diamonds! However, they all preferred the plainer one on my left hand, behind the diamond. That's the one that counts! I heard a lot of news about everyone.

I am so glad to hear that you are doing so well. I sure would be proud to pin on your bars. I love you!

I read what you wrote about your "Dark haired Greek" to my parents, and my Mother says: "What? Dark haired freak!" Thanks a lot Mom!

By the way, my painting looks better to me today. I have forgotten about the hard spots. Your Mother is a very good teacher, and her paintings are professional. Warning! Mine are not. Take care of yourself Honey. I love you so much. Love, Brent.

March 4, 1966, Quantico, VA: Dearest Brent, Good evening Darling. Your letters sound as if you are keeping busy. They are beginning to step up the pace here just a bit.

This last week we spent two days in the field for war games. They issued us blanks and sent us up against the School Demonstration Troops. They put them in prepared positions, usually at the top of a hill, broke us up into squads and told us to go get them. We even went up against another squad in a night attack. Boy, if you think going up against machine guns is fun, and work for heroes, you are definitely crazy. It takes a lot of team work and just a pinch of luck. I did not get "killed," (I hope you are happy about that.) but my bunkie got it two times. He does not believe in moving from tree to tree and doing it extremely fast.

Next week we have a night war and will be up all that night. As long as I get on the assault team, it will suit me. I can't see sitting in a foxhole all night, just waiting.

I am glad to hear that you are ready to do battle. Just remember, Marines are taught to be aggressive. So you had better take warning yourself. What I would not give to get my hands on you. I have a lot of loving built up inside of me, Honey. Your letter seals my feeling that our reunion should cause a few sparks.

I miss you very much Kitten. I would love to have my arms around you right now and with nothing to think about, but ourselves. Does it sound like a second Honeymoon? Well, it had better, in fact it should be one hell of a lot better. (We understand each other better now.)

You just wait Darling, I want you so damn bad and love you so very much. Knowing you are there and behind me all the way has helped me more than you will ever know. Thank you very much Brent. I am a very lucky man.

Say Kitten, I would give an awful lot to be able to read again. I get to read a newspaper about once a week. I can't even listen to a radio, and boy, do I ever miss hearing the news. Love, Steve.

March 5, 1966, Quantico, VA: Dearest Brent, Good afternoon Honey. Well, one more day has passed. We had another hike this morning of nine and eight tenths miles. One platoon lost twenty-nine candidates out of thirty-six. They really move out down here. We made the entire route in under two hours. That is really moving out considering we carry combat packs, M14 rifle belt, and hard hat. Today I served as a radio man, at least it kept me up by the platoon commander, traveling is easier up there.

As you can see we, myself included, are really tired. It is a funny feeling being this way. It is a mental condition as well as physical. You just reach a point where you stop thinking and just do what you are told.

I got a 98 on our latest exam. That should help more than just a little. Now, if I do not screw up the final exam, I should have a fairly respectable grade; but you know the kid!

Hey Girl, I want you to know that you saved my hind end today. When the going got really tough, I kept thinking about you on our wedding night. Nothing else could occupy my mind the way my memories of that wonderful night did. It is wonderful to have a woman care for you enough to give herself freely to you. To realize that a man is just a man, and that she possesses a gift that only she can give, that makes a man something more than just an animal.

I know one thing Kitten, there is no other person in this world that I want to be proud of me as much as you. I know I will never share as close a relationship with anyone else. It is close because we have given freely of ourselves, knowing that we will sometimes be hurt, but that a stronger and more meaningful relationship will be the end result.

(The tears burning behind Brent's eyes made it a challenge to read and type this silent tribute to their marriage.)

March 10, 1966, Quantico, VA: Dearest Brent, Good evening Darling. One very tired Marine is talking to you tonight. We are taking the last of our physical conditioning tests at the present. I hope to show a lot of improvement in each event.

Monday, we had a night war exercise. We were lifted by helicopter out into the sticks. From there on in we had to fight our way to a particular hill, take it, and dig in. We stayed all night with one hour on watch and one hour off. During the night we beat off three attacks from other platoons and completely wiped out the fifth platoon by a couple of squads of our platoon.

Enough of that! I want you to know I want to hold you, and have nothing enter my mind but making you and myself completely happy. Darling, you have no idea how much I want to hold you. Lady, you are just beautiful. I want you Brent. I want to see you, smell you, touch you, and hold you close all night. Love, Steve.

March 11, 1966, Quantico, VA: Dearest Brent.
Good afternoon Darling. Well, it is a beautiful day in Virginia. It is really like summer here in the sunny South. I do not understand how anyone can stand it during July and August.

I heard a bobwhite singing this morning for the first time. The bobwhite has a very pretty song; it easily makes getting up in the morning worth the lack of sleep. I am going to make sure you hear its song before too much time goes by. With each passing day I look forward more and more to Pensacola and flight training. I guess I will make the class in both math and physics. At the end of it all are my wings, I hope.

We received our uniforms for graduation today. There is quite a bit of work that has to be done on it yes; but, at least I have got it. (There was no sign off to this letter. He must have been very tired. This was the last letter from Quantico.)

N

Information regarding graduation was communicated via telephone. The date: March16 and March 17, 1966, Graduation: Officer's Candidate School, Quantico, Virginia.

It was decided that Dad Martin would drive from New Hampshire to Quantico, Virginia to attend Steve's Commissioning Ceremony as a United States Marine Corps, Second Lieutenant. Dad and Mother Martin, Brent, another family member and friend arrived at Quantico the evening before the ceremony.

Now this is where Brent recalled from Steve's letters the proper conduct for a Marine Officer. Such as: "No Marine Officer is allowed to kiss or hold hands with anybody while in uniform and in public." He also added: "Marines are the devil's own while in private, in or out of uniform!" Also, one can't help but go through a change in ones outward appearance and the way one reacts to situations." "I could seem different in some ways."

The place to meet Steve was lighted by street lights, and other people were in the area. Several of them were in uniform. Brent, remembering the above instructions saw a Marine purposefully striding in their direction. It was Steve, no longer a "potential" Marine; but a real, in uniform, Marine! He was transformed somewhat; and Brent was transfixed, taking him all in, and knowing it was him by the big "Martin" grin.

This is when Brent realized she should have warned their guests about conduct. She slowly walked towards him, relishing the moment, taking in the sight of him, and letting him lead the interaction of the moment, their reunion!

Brent was aware that Mother and Dad Martin were quietly waiting a few steps behind her and that their guests were there also. Suddenly, she heard Mother Martin say: "Wait!" But the guests rushed by her, giggling and running to engage Steve in a two-on-one bear hug.

Steve and Brent's eyes were locked upon each other. Steve disengaged himself from the enthusiastic greeting to stride towards Brent. He was allowed a short leave after the ceremony and his brief greeting was made up to her the next day on the drive home, as she nestled in his arms.

Brent doesn't remember much about the graduation ceremony; but has relished for years the pictures of Mother Martin and herself pinning on those shiny Second Lieutenant bars.

Quantico: Mother & Wife Pinning On The Second Lieutenant Bars.

March, 1966, Moultonborough, NH: Let the celebration begin! Steven W. Martin was now an Officer in the United States Marine Corps and on his way to be a Naval Aviator.

On the evening of the great party at his parent's house, Steve was welcomed home by aunts and uncles, grandparents, cousins, friends and neighbors, and even Brent's parents, were there to welcome him home.

For a while Steve and his friends were in an intense conversation aside from the main party. There were different branches of the military represented there with each one defending their choice of service. Brent was sure Steve presented the best case for his choice of the Marine Corps.

Steve was so intense that he seemed to barely notice the black lace dress Brent was wearing for him. The transition back to civilian life, after three months of intense training, was probably quite an adjustment even though he and she may not have realized it at the time.

The leave time went quickly. Mother and Dad Martin surprised them with a better replacement for the old car Brent had struggled with while Steve was gone, thus revealing why they told her not to register the old car. They packed the car with the necessities for setting up a home together near his new duty station: the Naval Air Station at Pensacola, Florida.

There was a two week stop over back at Quantico before he received his orders to report to Pensacola. They rented a motel room in Alexandria, Virginia. The highlight of the delay to Florida was a visit with other Marines to the Aviation display at the Smithsonian Institute in Washington, D.C.

Unfortunately, upon arriving in Pensacola, the "new" car was broadsided at an intersection. Steve received a bruise on his head; and Brent would carry that memory for the rest of her life, as she became what is known as a "back seat driver." It was not the way Steve wanted to report to his new base.

Steve's injury turned out to be minor. A new car was purchased, and a very nice duplex with a great landlord, was rented. Of their three years of marriage, the year and one-half they would live there, was the longest they would actually live together, before he left for Vietnam.

There were good times in Pensacola. Other young couples and singles also, became friends and were sharing the same experiences and excitement of becoming Naval Aviators. Steve's parents came to visit and enjoyed a tour of a carrier ship and the beautiful sandy beaches of the Florida Panhandle. Every weekend Steve and Brent went to a telephone booth to call home, to both sets of parents, to let them know the latest. Yes, a telephone booth! Second Lieutenants needed to watch the budget; and, cell phones were unheard of at that time.

Brent attended a Wives Indoctrination Tour. Each wife was presented a certificate with their name that read:

"U.S. Naval Aviation Schools Command. This is to certify that Mrs. S. W. Martin has successfully completed the WIVES' INDOCTRINATION TOUR and is henceforth authorized to give Advice, Sympathy, and Encouragement to those undergoing the rigors of The Naval Aviation Schools Command. Awarded this 2nd day of June, 1966. Signed by Commanding Officer."

The rigors, yes. The worst night of Brent's life, up to that time, was when Steve did not come home one whole night. There were no phone calls to the landlord, no one came by to explain. Nothing, all night long.

Finally, in the morning there was a knock on the door. It was Steven! Still dressed in uniform with all of his flight gear in hand. He was quite bewildered when Brent embraced him and burst into tears. "You mean no one sent you a message?!"

Brent wasn't sure whether "no message" was better than what the actual message would have been. The message would have been that the plane his instructor and he were flying had to land in Jackson, Mississippi, due to some problem with the plane. The repairs were completed the next day, and they flew back to Pensacola. Ironically, Jackson, Mississippi was where Steve was born when his father had served in the military during the Second World War.

On the 11th day of August, 1967, now First Lieutenant Steven W. Martin, U.S.M.C. was designated a Naval Aviator. Steve received orders to Jacksonville, N.C. to complete training as a helicopter pilot.

They lived there for three months, more or less. Housing was difficult to find for short timer military couples. The place they found was marginal, but they were together and made the best of it. There were visits from other young couples in the same situation.

The three months went by quickly and Steve received orders to go to Vietnam.

AFTER 2 DAYS SURVIVAL TRAINING

THIS IS WAR

Chapter 7

This Is War

December 13, 1967 was Christmas Day in a home, by a lake in Moultonborough, NH. It was Steve's last leave before going to Vietnam.

The Christmas tree was decorated, presents wrapped and under it. The aroma of a holiday meal was in the air. The family gathered and assumed the mood of normalcy; although, it was not normal to celebrate Christmas on Brent's birthday. And, it was not normal to say good-bye to your son or your husband any day; but, especially a few days before Christmas, to go to war!

After the festivities were over, Steve drove into town. Upon his return he exclaimed how surprised he was to see the stores open and the town bustling with people. It had worked! All of us had made it work! Christmas was a feeling and a celebration of a life that gave us hope and peace on earth, not just a date on the calendar.

THE

PARTY

BEFORE

GOING

TO

VIETNAM

12/17/1967

CAPTAIN

MARTIN

LEAVES

FOR

VIETNAM

Within a few more days the family drove to the airport and following Steve's example, remained composed. Steve and Brent exchanged one last glance as he turned, and walked to the gate to board his flight.

N

Steve had made arrangements for Brent to live with his parents before he left for Vietnam. It was a welcome situation for her, and put her closer to a medical clinic where she went to work.

N

December 25, 1967, Okinawa: Dear Folks, Merry Christmas everyone! I am now in Camp Hanson, Okinawa. We arrived here yesterday morning at Kaden A.F.B. We flew here by way of Anchorage and Japan. The trip lasted about sixteen hours and was by a commercial airline.

I found Buzz the night after I arrived in Treasure Island. We stuck close to the base because of the out of this world prices. Treasure Island sits in San Francisco Bay about half way between Oakland and San Francisco. It cost ten dollars for a one way cab trip to either city.

We met up with five other officers at Travis A.F.B. December 23rd. Our flight was delayed by twelve hours, so all of us hit one of the local bars in one of the small towns outside of Travis. Boy, what a send-off we had! Most of the people had never seen Marines before and never seven altogether. We managed to buy six rounds of our own, and the next ten or so were all free. It was a good Marine type good-bye party. They gave us a send-off I will not soon forget.

We left Travis 0200 on December 23rd. Nine hours later we hit Anchorage, Alaska. At nine degrees below and half pass dark, we were glad to see that go by the boards. Japan was just a piece of land in an awfully big ocean. However, Mount Fuji is truly beautiful. It stands alone in an entire range of mountains covered from top to bottom with snow. After thirteen hours of darkness and two pretty poor meals; we were glad to see Okinawa pass under our wings. This place is entirely different from anything I can think of to give you a mental picture.

The terrain is extremely rough as in a moon scape; and the earth is quite red, like our southern soils. There are plenty of trees, but they are all very small and look like the Japanese dwarf garden trees. The rocks and hills are very sharp and brittle looking; because I suppose, due to the lack of glacial action. Also, one feels like a giant sat down in a land where he is just a little too large to fit. The roads are narrow, the houses are very small, and of course, the people are small.

The people here seem very poor. There is very little land level enough to cultivate; everything is up and down. Most of the people work either for the military or some job aimed at the military. You see shops of all sorts, selling Japanese or U.S. goods; but, no fields or livestock. If the military ever pulls out, these people will be sunk.

Another interesting thing is that you seldom see anything purely Okinawan. Food is U.S., Japanese, or Chinese. Same for manufactured goods. These people seem to lack a culture of their own. The result is a culture that is Japanese and part Western.

Well, I am going to sign off for a while. Do not write me here as I will be going down south in a couple of days. I think of you a lot. Steve.

December 28, 1967, Okinawa: Dear Brent, Just a postcard to tell you that I am fine, except missing you. I have a long letter started, but I am waiting for free postage. Steve.

December 29, 1967, Vietnam: Dearest Brent, Good evening Baby! Well, I hope everything is going alright with you. I am sorry about the long silence, but it was really necessary. The long trip to my squadron is finally over. There are quite a few familiar faces here in HMM-362, known as The Ugly Angels. In case you are wondering we fly the good old UH-34.

The rains arrive today, and brother is it cold!! Get me an electric blanket. Make it a fairly small one so as to fit a cot. They keep you warm, dry your clothes, and keep your bedding dry. I am really serious, Kitten: get it double quick. Some way to fight a war, huh? Electric fans, TV, radios, and refrigerators are common place. I am living with five other officers in a "hutch" which is a hut without walls.

I hope to get some money tomorrow afternoon. I will send some directly home to you, Kitten. What you do not need, put in our bank account. We should build that back up to a good solid level.

All of us start flying tomorrow which is good. We have been sitting on our tails too long. Besides, the fighting has dropped off in our area. Need to get back into the swing of things during the lull.

We are listening to Hanoi Hanna. Boy, are they working on how we are not backed at home, and the idea that the Vietnam war is really Johnson's war. It is something to listen to this coming from people urging you to hear the message from home sound different. She also reads letters taken from American dead. People listen to her as she plays good music and puts out some good scoop. If she says they are hitting some place, you can count on it. What really hurts are the irresponsible statements you hear at home. Believe me, they really use these statements for all they are worth.

Oh well, that is the way the ball bounces. Say Baby, did you know that I love you very much. I hope you are spending your time the best way possible. I feel as if something good is being accomplished by my being here. Advance yourself Kitten; work and play like each day is your last. I am going to hit the rack. I love you so very much Darling, and I miss you. Steve.

N

No letters written to Steve from Brent or from Steve's parents were found until the one dated June 30, 1968. They were probably lost in country, or when his sleeping quarters were flooded when he was aboard a carrier ship. Letters received from Steve are continued here as each one was saved, and cherished for years. Steve's possessions were delivered home from Vietnam after his death.

N

January 1, 1968, Vietnam: Dearest Brent, Good evening Kitten. Well, I hope you are all having a good New Year's Eve. We are having rain and cold weather. The mud is half way to your knees. Everything is very dirty including ourselves. No sweat, we can get around that alright.

Half of my gear "turned" up lost. My flight gear, etc. got misplaced somewhere between Okinawa and Da Nang. Everything in my sea bag is now probably keeping some V.C. (Viet Cong) warm. Do not worry as I have replaced the gear. I just hope I will not have to pay for the flight gear.

I have finally been paid our back pay. Most I have left on the books, but I am sending some home. I am really sorry it took so long, Kitten. From now on you should not have that problem.

I have found several good deals on cameras, radios, and tape recorders. I have also run across some really unbelievable things in the firearms field. When I begin sending such things home, you may be required to pay a tax on them. I hope to get hold of a catalog that has china and silverware. Not too much else to report really. The weather has kept most of the operations in low gear.

These people seem larger and more robust than the Okinawan people. The land is really something to see. The lowlands are quite level and the mountains seem to spring directly up out of nowhere. These are really he-man mountains and they also appear quite new being high and very sharp looking.

The Highway One you hear so much about is a gravel road. A lot of the bridges have been blown. Traffic moves along at about thirty miles an hour. That is a bone jarring ride believe me!

The earth is a real red color and a lot of the land near the coast is under some sort of agricultural endeavor. There appears to be some amount of livestock, but mostly of poor quality.

You get the feeling that this country has a lot to offer her people and the rest of the world. Such a lot of good can be accomplished here by rolling up our collective sleeves and going to work. You have to start at the bottom of the ladder and improve the lot of the average citizen. Increase the farmer's ability to upgrade his produce, improve transportation and education, and train various skilled laborers. After we win this war, we can really do so much here. The Reds are not interested in seeing the people's lot bettered. Vietnam is a rung in the ladder of world domination. These people have a right to better themselves to the best of their ability. None of this business of governmental control in every aspect of your life. Our government is not always the best in this respect, but so far it has not reduced people to the level of ants.

Oh well, I am going to hit the rack now. Send that electric blanket as soon as possible. All my love Kitten. Say hello to everyone. Steve.

Well Kitten, guess what. The post office was closed by the time I got there. I also received dislocation and the rest of our travel pay. I will send some home, so put some in the bank, you hear! Our plans are too big to have anything except a solid foundation.

Nothing much else to report. Chow is good, and we get all we want to eat. Things are pretty damp right now and cold. When you fly it is really cold, so hustle that electric blanket up. Have got to get that money order and mail you this thing. Take it easy, Steve.

January 5, 1968, Vietnam: Dearest Brent, Good evening Kitten. I hope everything is fine with you and the folks. Things are good here; the food keeps getting better, and the flying is great! I flew on my first medevac about fifteen minutes ago. The feeling is simply wonderful knowing you helped in some small way in saving a life. I had just come in off the range where I had been practicing with my pistol so that I would be good enough to kill with it, and in the next fifteen minutes I helped, maybe, save a life. War is a very curious thing. It is always poking at a person's nature, stretching and turning it, looking for weak spots. People act in the strangest ways. Their reactions to a situation may be good, but their everyday behavior changes.

Today was a beautiful day with lots of sun, which makes it fairly warm for once. The country here is really beautiful, being very lush and green looking. The people are mountain people who are very small and dark. They look like young kids or real old men. I guess their life treats them very harshly. Mostly they do manual labor in and about the base. They live in seemingly orderly laid out villages that are quite different from the lowlanders. They must kill a lot of meat, for their land does not appear well suited for farming. Even so, almost every little creek is damned up and has its share of rice paddies.

They use very small crossbows to hunt with. A person can pick up one of these small crossbows for a few dollars. One would make an interesting addition to my collection of odds and ends.

I have found the perfect gift for you Kitten. I think it would be one of the last things you would expect, but I know you will love it. As soon as I get the necessary money, it will be swinging your way. Better start guessing, Kitten.

It goes without saying that I miss you badly, Darling. There is nothing like a warm woman on these cold nights. Just kidding darling, then again, I don't think I am. Will I ever be glad to see you again. It seems like ages, doesn't it? You and I are really going to town once I get this particular tour done up brown. It is really too bad to wish an entire year away like that. It is actually a crime to wish a year gone out of your life; yet nearly everyone does it.

I hope you have reached the same conclusion I have, Kitten. Each and every day must be used to the best possible advantage. Nothing is ever really truly perfect, yet nothing is ever really all bad.

Th only time I feel anxious about the time I have left here is when I think of you and the folks. My time here, I feel, is being well spent. I feel in many ways things could be done faster and much more efficiently; yet I feel I belong here in this country doing my small bit.

I realize that being married to a person like myself is not the easiest thing in the world. Somehow, I feel apart from many people here. Most are here because this is where they ended up.

They started out to become an airline pilot through military training and ended up here. I started out headed for here and became a pilot because of the extra challenge. I wonder which of us is the wiser and on whose family does the heaviest burden fall? I know I am happier being me. If you can stand my chasing after such things and not always "the good life," than I guess I am the luckiest.

How about that Kitten? I guess you will have to wait for me to explain that particular little point to you. Wait until I get home; I have enough material to lecture for six months without letting up. Are you in for it? Seriously, people are dam interesting when you stop to look at them close enough and long enough. Marines are especially interesting simply because they are tougher and are subject to more strain than the average person.

It is interesting, sometimes disquieting, to watch people change before your eyes. You would be very sad to see "the happily married man" hit the entertainment houses in Okinawa. Even I was surprised, and I was expecting it. There is something very sad about the entire thing. So many chasing something he can't catch, with girls they would not even look at in the daylight. I feel sorry for these people in a way; yet for all their noise, they lack what you and I have found Kitten. The knowledge that what they are or were, will be remembered by someone, no matter what happens. To be remembered as a man; or something less by even a whore, is important when you are going to war.

These people lack the feeling that they are something either in their own, or in their wives eyes. So, why waste our time worrying about this aspect of other people's lives. It is just a fact of life, I guess.

The entire point of the above is that although you and I have separate aspects to our lives; mine being lost in my own thoughts, we have reached an understanding between us that has transplanted the "I" with "we," yet have left more than enough room for individual direction and movement. It all means that I love you too much to do something like that to you or myself. My being here has a lot to do with the love we share.

Had enough? My feelings were not meant to be placed on something as cold and unfeeling as this piece of paper, Brent. I am saving most of the words for the time when we are together again. My feelings for you run very deep and very true. Saying the fact again and again does not make the time pass any quicker, so I say simply that I love you with all my heart and soul. Steve.

January 12, 1968, Vietnam: Dearest Kitten, Good evening Darling. Hope everything is going simply terrific with you and the folks. I am just beginning to get enough gear to make life fairly normal again. I would appreciate some white wool socks, about four pair will be just right. This exchange system has a really unbelievable selection of radios, cameras, watches, etc. but, you can't buy more than one bar of soap at a time and most articles of clothing are hard to come by.

Since I have not had a chance to complete my check-in, I hope you are addressing all mail with simply my squadron. Otherwise, the mail gets here a lot slower. According to the short-timers, it takes about three weeks for your first mail to arrive after your first letter. The mail moves rather slowly on our end.

As I have said before the flying here is really a lot of fun. As long as you come home, no one bitches too bad. Today was a beautiful day. The first warm one we have had. I had the squadron duty today so I missed out on the flying.

I have been able to see most of the places you have read and heard about on the news. Laos and North Vietnam I have seen in the distance. We picked a medical evacuation up right on the border of Laos. When we asked about where "Charlie" was, we were told not to fly over the river forming the border. Take that any way you want.

It is amazing how the time passes here. I can truthfully say that I have no concept what day of the week it is, normally. I will have to start marking the days off. The only problem being that days really mean nothing. It is work accomplished that really means a lot. Work and time interacting, are the true measure of a life. Here in Vietnam seeing people working, which appears all the time, bear this point home. How much work can they put out in the period of their lives allotted to Vietnam? How much work can they do before they need sleep or food? That is what is important.

See what I mean? I have any number of lectures to give. I would not trade places with you for the world. Besides, I like being the one on top! I bet that you do no show that little statement to everyone!

I had better close now and get some sleep. Love you a lot Kitten. Say hello to everyone for me. Steve.

January 5, 1968, Vietnam: Dearest Kitten. Good evening Darling. Hope things are going well for you and the folks. I have been ground bound the last few days. Just sitting on my hands. A really disgusting way to spend one's time. Hope things have been more productive for you.

I have not got my pay yet for the last two weeks. So it might be a while yet before I am able to buy that gift for you. Do not worry as you will get it in time. Time is one thing I have a lot of right now. You tend to forget about dates, etc. They really mean so very little.

Looks like this letter is going to take some time to get finished. I just happened to think that I have not told you much about what type of flying I am doing. We do a lot of resupply, transferring of troops, medevacs, and recon work. It can be putting Recon Marines, Special Forces, etc. out in "Indian" country; picking up their wounded and dead, and finally the rest of the team with what information they have gathered. Just a word about all of this, do not worry about "Charlie" shooting any aircraft out of the sky; he is the world's worst shot. Even I have got my seat high enough to see where I am going.

The grunts give us a bit of shit now and then, but we have no problem with the average trooper. He knows who brings his chow and mail, and who will have his tail into the hospital when he gets hit. Medevac is probably the most satisfying mission over here for me; to haul someone's tail out of trouble and maybe save his life. The second most satisfying is to get Charlie in a position where you can knock him on his tail for good.

At the present I am detached from my regular squadron to a base up near the DMZ. There are just two birds with our crews. We are getting a few hours resupplying the various outposts near here. By the way, I am way over next to the Laotian border and not close to Leatherneck Square.

There are many things wrong over here, but this place and these people are worth helping. At least, we are trying to help, not sitting on our hands wondering how to do the job the most intelligent way, and whether it is really our job to do. Charlie is going to get knocked on his butt when he tries a large scale fight. We are just too strong.

A lot more work has to be done with small units working over every inch of ground. Those hills and valleys are going to be taken by small groups of men moving over them day and night. One thing at a time, first the hard line regiments, etc. and then what is left. Special forces do a lot of work with hired troops. Those mothers earn every cent they get. Teams of about eight are dropped out in Indian country to look for Charlie. It is not unusual to lose an entire team before they get out of the zone. They are tough mothers; they go out again and again until they finally buy it. I do not think many get to enjoy old age benefits. As you can see, I really have it fairly easy. All I have to do is fly, which I love anyway. Steve.

January 20, 1968, Vietnam: Dearest Brent, Guess what happened today! I got relieved from the detachment I was on, and I received my first mail. Boy, I did not realize how much mail means. When I knew I was not going to get any, I just never looked or thought about it at all. Believe me, it is great to hear from you. You all have the right idea; just write about the things you are doing and what you are thinking.

Well, I am glad to hear that everything is going so well for all of you. I am really amused about you Brent. I have no doubt that working at the medical clinic can be interesting, Do not worry about Dad. He is just finding out what it is like to have the women work for him.

Tell Mom that it must be the part of her that came over here with me, that makes sure I wash behind my ears no matter how tired I am.

We fly here at odd times, but mostly in the mornings. However, we are awakened an hour before our brief time. When we are detached, we stand-by to be launched at any time we are needed. In other words, we haul supplies until something like a medevac comes up. Then we drop everything and do the medevacs.

Also, when I say we are detached, I mean at least two of our birds will go somewhere and work for the grunts completely separate from our squadron. They feed us, house, and see that we have fuel, etc. and we do their helicopter work for them.

By the way, one of the HAC's (Helicopter Aircraft Commander) told me today that I am now considered a broken in H2P (Helicopter Second Pilot) I have seen it, and I can be counted on. You never can see all the enemy has to offer, but they are sure you will remain cool most of the time. (Note the "most!")

Most of the HAC's last about six months, and then their nerves go bad, and they get a desk job. Of course, counting co-pilot time means they fly about nine or ten months over here. They fly some, all of their tour in most cases, but the last few months they usually cut the time way back. You know, the duty four hours a month. (Captain Martin was in his tenth month when he crashed.)

I met my platoon Commander from OCS, (Officer's Candidate School) and I would never have known him, but he remembered me. He asked me if I remembered him, and he flustered me so I could hardly say "hello." It is hard to forget the air those people built around themselves back at Quantico. I am sure my platoon Sergeant could have me doing push-ups before I remembered myself.

I can't say that we get that cold here Kitten, but when you combine the humidity and the cool breezes, the results are very cold people. The birds (helicopters) have a coat of frost some mornings. At two thousand feet and doing ninety knots it gets mighty cold.

As you would expect, the things I would like best are homemade cookies, etc. Do not send a lot as we are infested with rats and anything left overnight just feeds the local vermin. We buy all our food in cans or plastic containers.

I do not want you to worry about spending money on new clothes, Kitten. That is what the advancement is for. Your personal allowance is to buy whatever you want to, and the advancement is for new clothes, shoes, etc. Do not feel bad about it as that is what money is for. Buy to your heart's content!

I was "up there" today, but we could not go in because they were being hit hard at the time. During the rest of the attack, I was there. For three days we brought the wounded and the dead in from the hills. Charlie is going to pay dearly for every wounded and dead Marine. I have seen too many young Marines cut to pieces. If they are awake, they never say much of anything; no matter how bad the wounds. I have seen such brave men with broken bodies and the pain stricken faces of boys. The first day I did my job with tears streaming down my face. In the next two days, I have had such a hatred replace that feeling of uncontrollable sorrow. Charlie is going to pay dearly for every American, every Marine, hurt by him. This war is no longer just an American war. It is my war.

Charlie has extended peace feelers and he is going to try to give us a couple of really stiff blows. The idea being that the knowledge of the heavy cost of this war will be brought home to the American people. He also can then point to a victory in the last battle of the war; thereby implying, he won the war because of winning the last battle. Lastly, his bargaining power would be stronger at any peace table. I just wish more people could see this country and the people. The potential is terrific! Why talk ourselves into selling an entire country into slavery; not only one country, but an entire region of the world. How can you rationalize your way out of this? Everything is not roses here for these people, but we must fight this just as hard as we have fought other wars.

Fight not only in other lands, but our own as well. Not just money, but sweat from an American's brow, and whatever the people endure, our advisers must endure also. What happened to the good old fashion Yankee mind? Has it gone milky with soft living? We need people who have their feet on the ground and their minds on the task at hand. People who know what the dawn looks like.

Wake up people! I am awake for the first time in a long while. My task now is simple, win this war, and we will in time! The war is mine because I believe in our reasons for fighting, and my people have been hurt by those people on the other side! Steve.

January 28, 1968, Vietnam: Dearest Kitten. Good Kitten. Hope everything is going well with you. Things are busy here per usual. I have not had a day off for three weeks. We work here seven days a week, from before sunrise to well after dark. The time passes the fastest this way.

I still have not found time to get to the P.X. (store) to buy your gift. I have it picked out and priced, but I have not got it yet. Do not worry, it will arrive when you least expect it. I am sure you will simply be surprised beyond words. It is something you have deserved all your life. I am glad I could buy the most important person in my life something like this. I had hoped to get it to you for Valentine's Day. Now it looks like I will be able to get it only after that date, but the feeling is definitely there darling.

You know it is strange to be flying along looking at some of the world's most beautiful landscape and have it suddenly disappear in a cloud of flame or a tower of dust and smoke. Actually, it is so much like life; the violence always luring beneath a layer of respectability, waiting for an unsuspecting moment to burst upon the scene.

Several people have all sent letters for which I am very grateful. Do not feel so sorry for me, people. I do not like war, but this is where I belong. I realize that all of this is hard on my family, but it is what is right. I feel this war is necessary, and would not I be one hell of a person if I had opinions as strong as mine, and I was not willing to do any more than talk. I could not let someone else fight a war I feel is right when I am able to fight also.

Do not listen to war stories for they are just that: stories. There is no sense in worrying about things over here. You just pray you will always be able to do your job. There are many things more important than just keeping your tail safe. Being safe at any price is not worth the cost. You learn the many shades of words like "courage" and "gallant." Things here are often ugly; yet men go out day after day, knowing that their chances are very often slim.

Yet, these people go out and do their jobs in a cool, professional manner. That is courage when you know no one will pin any medal on you or even say too much more than: "Well done" No flags or drums; just brave men fighting the war day-by-day and hour-by-hour. When you think about it, this far surpasses the "story book" type of courage. You can sleep a little better knowing such a thing can still be found in our time. As an American, I am very proud of our nation's young men. They truly know the price of freedom. Steve.

January 29, 198, Vietnam: Dearest Kitten. Well, today was really an awful one. I do not believe I did one "little" thing right all day. The "big" things, no sweat. I goofed again and again on the things you just naturally do correctly. I am really ticked! That will change and quickly!

I hope you are putting some money out of the allotment check in the savings account. I want you to get those clothes and all those things you have gone without for so long. However, we must save a bit every pay period just to keep in practice. We will not be have-nots worrying about where the money for our kids' education will come from. I refuse to let money run through our fingers like sand. Saving and planning build you as well as your bank account.

I am not interested in money solely as money or as the purchasing power it has, but as the independence it provides.

I want us to live our life the way we want, Kitten. Hard work and hard play; people serious about the things that occur about them. Someday that will apply to us Kitten. We will walk our own way with no gates or fences to clutter and channelize everything and everyone. I know we will do things our way!

I only know that I am happy, Brent. I really found the girl for me when I found you. Even our romance was not the norm. God, I am lucky to have you. You tie the loose ends all together, Kitten. Not really an object in my life, but a part of it. You are like a lovely scent in the air that is always there. Love you very much Kitten; very much!

The days are getting hotter now, but the nights are still darn cold. By the way, the blanket has arrived. Now everything is warm at night the way it should be. I really do not need a lot of things. The simple things are the hardest to get; socks and underwear are impossible to get.

Well, I am going to wash up and hit the hay. Another day, another dollar. Say hello to everyone. Everything is fine here. Keep them fine on the home front. Steve.

February 2, 1968, Vietnam: Dearest Brent, Good evening Kitten. Hope everything is going alright with all of you. Things are really busy for us right now.

According to what we have been told, Charlie has lost ten thousand killed and three thousand people held in the newest offensive. We have lost around a thousand people. All his advances are breaking his back. The reason Charlie has done so well it that he is really hitting the ARVN very hard. Hue has been a hot spot for the last three days. The ARVN fought with them for two days, and then we landed Marines inside the city. Still hot up there. Since we have taken over, things are really speeding up.

Dearest Brent. It is now February third. As you no doubt know by now Charlies is really getting his butt soundly kicked. He bit off way more than he could chew. Charlie did fairly well against the ARVN's, but he is doing nothing but getting himself soundly beaten when he comes up against U.S. troops. The odds where I am is running about one to thirty. The information we got is thirteen thousand NVA to one thousand two hundred allied troops. Those odds speak for themselves. We are breaking Charlie's back. His bid for a strong position at the peace table has been put down for the present offensive. I hope people at home are using their heads about this thing. Charlie tried for all he was worth to get a victory somewhere. So far he has failed. Do not believe this means Charlie has lost more than a battle because he has not. Charlie can still win if we listen to some people or give up all at the peace table.

Why, when so many have died for a good and just cause, would some sell it all for power or some other equally poor reason. Some people will attach their wagon to any star as long as it serves their ends. They would sell their own country down the drain.

Well Kitten, enough of this. I am too close to the other side of the fence. You do not sit there sating how bad everything is, yet do nothing to better the situation.

Several people I know from the training squadron and New River have checked into HMM-362. Some of our guys have gone to Okinawa for a much needed R&R.

Boy, what I would not give to be able to see you Brent. We are kept busy most of the time, however, during those lack times and at night, I miss you very much. I would give a lot to be able to get my hands on you. Your lovely face and figure haunt me Kitten. I would like to talk to you, but I would also like to hold you in my arms again. I need to show you love even if it is only with words! You had better be all dressed up when I come home. Your nicest outfit and some alluring underwear Kitten.

We will make this a really terrific reunion. Something we will always remember. I bet our love will reach a new all-time high! Not only because it has been a long while, but because we have matured along with our love. Each day I learn anew how much you and your love means to me. The depth of feelings between us never fails to amaze me. It far surpasses a merely physical attraction, which I also have for you kitten. I can honestly say I have never wanted any other woman more than I want you. I want to grow with you. First in our personal lives, then with our family and to finally grow old together.

That is the way I want to spend my life Kitten. Building a good life for us, our family, and those around us. Our "good life" has a lot of "giving" in place of a lot of "getting" only. My job is going to give me more than money alone. Our marriage is going to give us more than security. Our family is going to give us more than just worries, but love and joy. It won't be a means of racing the people next door. Some people put their values on things. Doing things because every-one does it, does not hack it with us Kitten. We are going to have our own "good life' and a darn full one at that.

Well, Kitten, I guess I will heat some water and shave. Everything is fine over here. Hope things are going well for you. Steve.

N

Peter Pohl, a friend of Steve, contributed this letter on March 13, 2019. It was written to Peter by Steve, dated February 4, 1968, Vietnam.

Dear Pete, Good to hear from you, "Boy!" Hope things are beginning to take shape for you. I know what working without a challenge is like. Remember, while working as an assistant plumber, I dug an awful lot of holes in our good New Hampshire earth. Just never settle for what you do not want, and you will wind up on the right road.

Brent has written about you and Rich seeing that she gets out and about a bit. I really want to thank you for that Pete. Being a "nice" girl and with her husband being overseas does not give her a lot of chances for an evening out. Once again, I really appreciate you guys giving her a good time.

Well, about what is going on over here. Needless to say my position is one of a very small cog in a very large wheel. Just the same, I have a very great feeling of accomplishment and involvement in Vietnam.

This country has simply terrific potential. Charlie has said that unless Vietnam becomes a communist state, there shall be no advancement. It is so easy to do nothing but destroy and never build anything. It does not mean anything to him if thousands die before the end he has selected is reached. According to them the end justifies the means. Years of standing still or moving backward, as a county, is alright if a communist state results.

The country itself is really beautiful. A coastal plain of between ten and thirty miles in width gives way to some of the world's most rugged mountains. Nearly every possible piece of earth is used on the coastal plain. Areas that are close to water are used to grow rice, and the dried ground is used to build their homes on and to bury their dead in. The graves appear to be huge buttons scattered all about as if by some giant's hand. The lands and homes look so neat and extremely well cared for. Of course, everything smells to the high heavens, but then, some of our cities have the same problem.

The whole idea being that these people seem to care and while they do not work as hard as us New Englanders, they work hard. They deserve the chance to live in a free country.

Six million of them chose the South over the North and moved below the 17th parallel at the end of the war with France. We can never be too big to bend over to help. Not only with military arms, but by bending our backs and sweating alongside them. We should not try to build the country of Vietnam in our own image, but as a free healthy state that stands on its own. Money is not the answer, sweat and a lot of hard work after a well thought out plan has been worked out and agreed upon. A lot of things are wrong over here, but they will not change by us pointing them out 10,000 miles away. The Reds would love the chance to change things.

The flying here is really great. Charlie shoots at you quite a bit, but he is the world's worse shot. By the way, we are facing mostly NVA here in I Corps. He is fairly well supplied and really quite well equipped. The idea of him using mostly U.S. weapons, etc. is pure con. Most of the weapons we capture bear Chinese or Russian markings. Most of his artillery consists of mortar and rockets. The rockets make a lot of noise, but they do not appear to be very accurate.

From what I have seen over here Charlie is really getting his tail waxed nearly every time he comes out to fight. The odds are really heavily in our favor. During the last NVA offensive at KheSanh and Hue, we have been killing them at a 11.5 to 1 ratio. I have been working at both KheSanh and in an about Hue, and I know we have not been losing a lot of Marines for the amount of shooting Charlie has been doing.

At first we let the ARVN'S screw around with Charlie up in Hue. After two days, we lifted marines into the old walled city just at dusk. The next morning Charlie started running.

The Huey's would catch a few crossing a river or open piece of land and really chew them up. Charlie is really paying for his try at catching us with our pants down. We just received word that Charlie has lost close to four hundred confirmed killed to twenty-seven Marines killed at Hue. Believe it or not that is pretty close to the truth.

Believe me a vicious rocket attack to the newspapers does not even get us to get out of the rack. The newspapers have been way out in left field as far as reporting the things I have seen. I guess they are trying to sell newspapers. One headline screamed that 25,000 men of the Airborne have gone to the aid of the Marines at Khe Sanh. I am sure the 26th Marines feel better now. After all, they are only surrounded by two NVA divisions, and the only Airborne or even Army unit is at least fifty miles away. By the way, we are whipping their tail even without the Army's help.

Enough of this crap. Just form your own opinions and base them on what you know as fact. I could not even talk to the average Joe about Vietnam for he has been told one thing, and I have seen something completely different.

Well Pete, thanks for lending me your ear. Keep watching for your chance to get rolling again. It is sure to come along. Steve.

Peter's note to Brent dated March 13, 2019: Despite so many years, this tragic loss of a great guy seems like yesterday. Regards, Pete.

N

February 6, 1968, Vietnam: Dearest Kitten, Good evening Honey. Hope everything is going well for you and everyone else. Things are going well here. Right now we are whipping Charlie at a terrific rate. For a while the old walled city of Hue was flying a Red battle flag. Once we received clearance to strike the city, that did not last long. We are really breaking Charlie's back now that he has come out into the open.

If we could send troops into Laos, we could really fix Charlie's little red wagon. I think I have labored the point enough. You no doubt get the point as I know what I see.

Well Kitten, how have you been? I bet you look simply terrific!! Would I like to be chasing you around the living room. Remember when I did that? I made it my life's work to get you to marry me. I am planning to have one hell of a reunion with you.

You know Kitten, I hope you are getting enough money. I also hope you are setting aside some money for savings. Also, use some to buy a few outfits to seduce your husband with. Steve.

February 8, 1968, Vietnam: Dearest Kitten, Well good afternoon Darling. We are having a cold rainy day here. You may be cold, but I am sure you are not mired in mud. Ceilings have been real low lately. The flying takes on interesting facets in this type of weather.

We like to fly above fifteen hundred feet when possible. In bad weather we go low level. That means flying around twenty feet off the deck. The idea being that at around a hundred and ten knots, Charlie will be unable to react before we are gone. Flying over rice paddies we really get low, and do a bit of bouncing around so Charlie can't figure out where we will be in the next second. This is also a good way to get Charlie if he pops up. We got three a little while ago. They were hot about downing a helicopter and got their ass waxed for their trouble.

Our hooch maid, a Vietnamese woman who works for us, came back today. During the latest offensive all Vietnamese were not allowed on base. By her actions she had a really hard time. The N.V.A./V.C. held her village, off and on, during the hard fighting. It is too bad to send us over here and not teaching us, at least, a little Vietnamese. There is so much she could probably tell us about herself and her country. I know she runs a great deal of risk by working for us. Who knows, she may be V.C. herself; but I doubt it. She smiles too readily and seems to be happy with things. Of course, we have taken great pains to be nice to her. I just hope she really is not a V.C.(Viet Cong)

I am glad to see that your clothes situation is getting fixed. I have spent a little myself. The first purchase was a 35-mm camera, good but not costing much, to use over here.

I am still looking for that gift I picked out for you. They changed the store around and when I finally managed to get there, the item was not displayed. Just hang on, it is worth it.

There are some really good deals over here for women's watches and jewelry. Do you want to trust me? The way I figure, now is the time to get you some jewelry. We may have a beat-up car, no house, and a small bank account; but my wife will wear jewelry just as chic as she is.

Find out how much a ticket to Japan would cost, Brent. We will do it on either my second or third R&R. That gives us around six to ten months to raise the loot. The pay jump to Captain would help a bit also.

Sorry to hear about our neighbor. Where was he when he got hit? We take the best possible care of our wounded over here. Our copters will go up against most anything to get the wounded back to help for them. Once we have them aboard it is, "balls to the wall," until we get them to help. Everyone on my end really knocks themselves out. I am sure the Corps will give him, like any other Marine, the best we have got. Well Kitten, I am going to chow. I will write again soon. Lots of love. Steve.

February 11, 1968, Vietnam: Dearest Kitten, Good evening! Things are starting to settle down a bit for us. We are cleaning up mostly. Charlie is not running anymore. He is digging in; actually playing our game. I think he is trying to put the pressure on our airfields and tie up troops while hammering away at Khe Sanh. Charlie is paying a price for his plans.

The weather has been very poor here and shows no signs of getting better. Charlie is facing an old fashion Marine: "Do you want to live forever?" attack. Charlie may be good, but he is not good enough to withstand that!

You know, you can really go broke saving money over here. Nearly everything costs less here. You may even end up sending money to me Kitten! There are diamonds, pearls, wrist watches, and Thai silk, the finest in the world.

Also, Thai silver and gold jewelry and china with silverware. I know I will get some things for you out of all this.

I have seen some really beautiful places. They simply can't be described. Beauty as we know it, in some ways, is on an entirely different scale than what we see here. In a good many ways Viet Nam resembles a moonscape. The villages are really beautiful from the air. I saw some sort of a holy place or royal tomb or something; but, it was tremendous. Their homes and nearly everything they touch their hands to reflect not only their country, but also their way of living in it. The buildings and garden plots are so painstakingly constructed and cared for. As if the days required to do something right are nothing as long as the building is done just so. The country seems as peaceful as these thing would indicate. It is always a physical shock to see a peaceful scene suddenly turn into a cloud of fire or a ball of dust.

At times it seems a mistake to have these people pushed into a driving, striving machine we call modern society. It comes to everyone sooner or later, I hope for the best. There is so much we can give these people. There is so much they can give us. They can give us the thing we have forgotten: hard work and rugged independence are worth more than all the material things. To be able to say with pride that I am a man and to know I am right. To realize that to be a man is more important than mere wealth and power. Manhood is not a name, but a way to live, a reason to do things. Young man, old man, all are satisfied with just one thing: that a man is still a man. Steve.

February 20, 1968, Vietnam: Dearest Brent, Good afternoon, Kitten, I hope things are going smoothly. Everything must have settled down, as much as the Martin household ever does.

Just read the February 9th issue of Time magazine. The article on Vietnam was not too bad. A couple of mistakes in basic facts, however.

The squadron is going aboard the boat, supposedly fairly soon. We should have a school trained officer pack up all our things and get them moved on schedule!

I believe I will be going on my first R&R (Rest and Relaxation) sometime in April. Most people get three R&R's per tour over here. I am thinking along the lines of just two for myself. I want to have enough money to really do some shopping and go to the places I want to see. Right now I want to go to Hong Kong and Thailand. Good places to shop and a chance to see some more of the culture of the Orient.

We have not been getting any mail for the last week. It is supposedly held up on Okinawa. Troops and badly needed supplies are over-taxing our transportation aircraft. We sure can stand getting the supplies. Nothing critical but there are some things we could use. We are really well taken care of. We have it great compared to servicemen in prior wars the U.S. has been involved in. No sweat!

I am spending money like it was nothing. The stuff we use looks like play money and you attach about the same importance to it. Ten dollars is not like spending green backs. However, we are also saving and should be well on the road to having a few of the things we have always promised ourselves: namely, a home and land for us to enjoy, and some really fine things to heighten our enjoyment.

How is your job coming along, Brent? What did you do with your hard earned cash? I hope your wardrobe was increased; remember always quality, never just quantity.

Love you a lot Kitten. Take good care of yourself, darling. You know you forget the strangest things, or maybe you remember the strangest things. Anyway, I know you must be something special because of the feelings I retain about you. You, flying, and my love for you are about the strongest attachments I have to life as it was back in the States. Give my love to everyone, Steve.

N

Seven letters from February 23, 1968 to March 17, 1968 followed the same vein about the rigors of war in Vietnam, missing family, Brent, and his pride in the United States Marine Corps.

N

March 17, 1968, Vietnam: Dearest Brent, Good evening darling. I am going to start sending things home the first of April. I have gotten very materialistic of late, haven't I! My reasons are sound, however, at no other time will we be able to get things as reasonable as we can now.

I am glad to hear that your job at the Clinic is going well. Keep up the good work. Love, Steve

N

Brent remembers the pleasure of receiving all the packages and appreciating his taste in things for their home. His mother was equally pleased with the gifts he had picked out for her. Included were 12-place table settings with accessory pieces, and bronze flatware sets with teakwood handles.

There was also reference of Brent saving money for a ticket to Japan to meet him for R&R. He set the travel dates as sometime in late September or October. Why this plan was shelved, Brent would never know. Would it have made a difference in the final outcome?!

March 29, 1968, Vietnam: Dearest Brent, Good evening Darling. How are you doing? Everything is okay with me. They grounded me again for having too many hours. Bugs me for them to do this. I need a lot more hours to perfect my skills. Besides being a good co-pilot over here is a demanding job.

Do you remember the Captain from flight training? He is over here now, and I flew with him yesterday on day medivac. It seemed odd to correct him when he made mistakes, as he had a problem with the radios. There was a lot of traffic and Charlie is usually jamming our communications. I ended up handling the radios and finally doing the flying. I am learning to do hundred knot approaches, no sweat. More than once I lost the Captain completely.

In other words he had no idea what was going on. I want a lot of hours so that when I make HAC, I will not have to wonder what is going on.

Well, enough of this shop talk. I want to make Hong Kong for R&R awfully bad. You should see the things that are available from the stores. This is the place I would like for us to go. Maybe we will go at some later date. Something to think about and plan for, huh?

Just got done at a party for two of our heavies who are leaving us. Had a bit to drink (not a wise idea) and watched a smoker (not very wise either) The girls were extremely good looking.

Right now one of the guys in my hooch is trying to explain to his wife what he did for five days and nights on R&R. He told her it took him two and a half days to buy books for me. (Now for reality ladies, from Brent.) Actually, he bought himself a beautiful Chinese girl for $15.00 for 24 hours and racked it out for five days. You should see her picture, she is a real knock-out!

Anyway, the old guy is getting a bit of what he deserves. She really is giving him hell! People are beyond me most of the time. He would "kill" her if she ran around on him.

Miss you a lot Brent. Love you lots. Steve.

April 10, 1968, Vietnam: Dear Brent, Good evening Darling. Things are fine here with yours truly and the rest of the Ugly Angels.

We are flying, and I am getting my share of hours, and I am happy as hell. I just got back from supporting the Marines relieving Khe Sanh. We flew medivacs, combat troops, and supply. That is the fourth operation we are supporting at the present time.

The causality rate has been very low for us on some operations. We are finding lot of the dead enemy that artillery and bombing have hit. The enemy has been badly out classed in various ground contacts.

I work out of the Navy forward hospital serving the entire operation, and talked to the doctor who had control of a field hospital during a battle. He remembers 35 U.S. civilians (teachers, CIA, agricultural experts) who were found with their hands tied and shot through the head. When you make judgements on the death of the V.C. officer by the Chief of Police, remember these Marines and American men and women who died that way. Also remember all the wounded and dead who have passed through this Doc's hands.

The doctor also wrote an eighteen page letter with all of the facts and figures praising the Marine Copter crews. Twenty minutes, night or day, good weather or bad, hot zone or not, we would have the wounded aboard and be headed out. At Ca Lu our reactions time was as low as seven minutes from the call for help, to man aboard, and headed out.

We share a bond with these people you can't understand. I have seen HAC"s who have had their planes shot to pieces, while getting in and out of a zone; break down and cry when a man dies on board his plane. There is always that feeling that he could have lived---if only. The Doc said only three men died in four weeks while waiting for us. He also said they would have died no matter if they were in the best hospital in the States. One of the Doc's prize moments was greasing a gook at around 2,000 yards with a.50 cal. machine gun. He said it made him feel a lot better. You feel good knowing that zip will never pull another trigger on another Marine.

We are going on the boat at the end of this week. We will be working with the Marine Landing force up North. We will be aboard ship for around three months. No change in address is needed. I have to eat and then fly, so I must finish this now. Take it easy Kitten. Say hello to everyone. Steve. P.S. We have been frozen at First Lt. because of the peace talks.

April 13, 1968, Vietnam: Dear Brent, Good evening Kitten. Have a good day today? I am getting packed for moving to the boat. Everything is torn up and spread to the four winds. Thank goodness I don't have too much as it makes it easier for me to get set to go.

I hope everything is going all right with you. Life is meant to live as full and as usefully as possible. Many times we must overlook the faults that others have, remembering a man's feet are truly made of clay. I have to remind myself of this fact every day.

So Kitten, how are you doing? Would like to have my hands on you right this minute. No good trying to palm me off on some unsuspecting girl. You and you alone are stuck with me.

I am very proud of the shape you are keeping our financial affairs. We should be able to seriously try to find a suitable house and land. God only knows, we will have so much gear we will need a house to store it in. The Steve Martin's will also have to have some serious talks concerning what profession we shall take on for good.

I must be getting old, but I want some solid plans for us to pursue. I am also going to be catching up on my homework. The idea of us having children now seems very important. I want something left from you and me and our enduring love. I really do love you my darling. After two and a half years of marriage my love for you has only grown. Steve.

April 15, 1968, Vietnam: Dearest Brent, Well here I am aboard the Iwo Jima Carrier, rocking back and forth. At present I am enjoying the milk, fried chicken, shrimp, movies with popcorn, and cold sodas.

We look awfully dirty, loud mouthed, and out-of-place. The Navy guys do not mess with us at all. We look too lean and mean and by far too well armed. In our squadron alone we have AK-47's, grease guns, Thompson's, M-16, M-14, and even a Swedish K submachine gun. All this besides our side arms and the more common arms. All in all, we do not look like people to screw with, and they are correct. We have moved right in.

Today was spent carrier qualifying some of our pilots. The Navy was very impressed with us and the professional manner we flew our aircraft. I get to fly tomorrow. Wonder what the Navy will think then?

Still shopping for our things. Some of your jewelry will be coming home with me. That way you will be looking forward to seeing me when I return. I am going to have to buy some boot polish and square myself away. Been a grub long enough.

I only plan to take two R&R's verses three. I do not seem to need as much rest as others. I seem to stand flying. No sense taking a duty R&R when someone else needs the rest.

Well Kitten, how is your job going? Glad to hear it is keeping you busy. Making your own money and spending it twice as fast, huh! I am very proud of the way you have kept our financial house in order, in fact, I believe you have straightened it up here and there. Well done! No doubt about it, I got myself a damn good wife!

My views on the "peace" are quite loud and profound. The American people are being misled and cheated. The American servicemen will pay with blood and tears. Charlie is fairly weak overall, but as soon as we take the pressure off, Charlie will regroup and hit us when and where he wishes. He will also use the fighting as a lever at the "peace" talks. Peace at what cost and to whom? Steve.

April 21, 1968, Vietnam: Dearest Brent, Everything is fine here. No fly today because of late watch duty. There seems to be no action here at all. I go on R&R in seven days, and I have almost no flight time this month. I hate sitting on my tail day after day.

The crew of an F-4 ejected right above the Carrier this evening. Both people landed within a half mile of the carrier. We picked them up almost as soon as they hit the water. The wingman gave us a victory roll after the people were picked up. The only reminder we have had in a week that there is a war going on. We are growing soft and rusty. Combat will be a shock after this. By the way, the crew of the F-4 is in fine shape.

A sailor fell overboard about an hour ago from one of the sister ships. The Navy can lose people and almost never fire a shot. Have a party and sailors fall into the sea like lemmings leaping off a cliff.

Read the latest "news" magazines. Dam things make me mad every time I open the cover of one of them. This week they were solving our "problems" over here. How I resent people who do not KNOW, giving advice.

Things are pretty mixed up in this world of ours aren't they Kitten. My ideals seem so simple and natural. Maybe they are naïve by today's standards, but I like them. It is like our relationship Darling. I married a girl I loved and plan to love and live with all of my life. No big thing to other people, but I found the girl that was meant to be mine and made her my wife. Nice and simple and straight forward sounding isn't it. It isn't as easy as it sounds. I must have had a lot of luck working for me also. Martin luck I guess, to get good women. I am really very proud of you Kitten. My own personal example of an ideal wife. The sailor was found in good shape! Steve.

April 27, 1968, Vietnam: Dear Brent, The flying is picking up; just when I am going on R&R. Sometime the 29th I should be arriving in Bangkok. I am looking forward to seeing the place and spending my money.

Thanks for the pictures of everyone. You look kind of natural holding your baby nephew in your arms, Brent. I am really thinking we should tackle that next Kitten. I really feel like taking on the responsibility. How about a son for the first one?

What are you thinking about right now Darling? I really do think we should stop disappointing the folks. They are waiting to spoil the hell out of the little monster. Just as if we have not been spoiled by their many kindnesses.

You know we have so many really tremendous dreams and goals. We have been so very lucky in that more that our fair share have come true.

You did not know your life was going to be so screwed up when you married me. Well anyway, you have seen a bit of this country of ours. Just enough to know you must see the rest. Should we see again most of what we have already covered? I would like to be stationed either in Quantico or on the west coast for my next stateside duty station.

You know Kitten, I miss those Friday night steak dinners and relaxing with you in our abode, no matter how humble. Steve.

May 4, 1968, Vietnam: Dear Brent, Well good afternoon Darling. My five days are now finished. I am back in Da Nang and the post R&R blues have set in. I met so many wonderful people in Bangkok and had such a great time. Needless to say, I spent lots and lots of money; had a steam bath, and danced with beautiful girls.

I do not know how it would work with you coming over here for one of my R&R's. The time is so damn short, and I would not be able to say good-bye to you. I did not realize how much I missed female companionship until I had a chance to remember the unique place they have in a man's life. The only love I have ever had is you Brent. I can kind of replace the feeling of tenderness a woman gives a man; but Darling, you are the only woman I can find happiness with.

Not one of those girls really interested me as far as partners in making love. I felt the warmth of female companionship, but I needed you. Damn, how would I ever say goodbye after finding you again. Damn Kitten, I just can't out run you at all. I need your love and understanding more than most men would ask of their woman.

Well, Kitten, there are some goodies coming. The dark jade ring size 7-1/2 is for my mother. The rest are yours. The opal ring is really special Brent. It took me two days to find and bargain for that stone. If you notice, the settings tend to be alike. This is because I picked the stone out first and then had them mounted in the simplest settings I could think of.

Everything you buy in Thailand is done by bargaining. You go into a store and sit before these long, enclosed glass cases containing all these beautiful gems. When you enter a shop they give you Thai beer (18% proof; tastes slightly green) coffee, or a soft drink. As long as you stay your glass is always full. One really feels like a "king."

I was greatly impressed by the Thai people. They are hard-working people, but seem to be the happiest I have ever seen. Bangkok has more new, really modern buildings going up. It seems funny to see modern buildings being put up by time honored methods. Bangkok is really quite a clean city. There are the bad sections, but our cities have them also. Their canals are actually open sewers. The main roads are well made and well lighted.

Needless to say the cab drivers are something else. All they seem to use is the gas pedal, steering wheel, and horn. Each person has to find his own way of enduring each cab ride. I prayed a lot. That way I could keep my eyes closed. I saw only three accidents, all minor, but I don't understand how.

We hired a taxi driver from our hotel. He showed us the sights and made us feel right at home. He seemed to know everyone and every point of interest.

Thai boxing is one of the most interesting things I have ever seen. The only thing you can't do is bite. Of course, the Thais are violently interested and bet heavily; as well as offer the fighter advice in between rounds. They rush up to ring side and berate the boxer, all of which he politely listens to. The actual fighting is done to music and they really go at it. Really exciting!

Incidentally, the charm bracelet and charms are gold. The woven gold necklace and bracelet, I thought, are beautiful. They should look beautiful on you. I am sending an order into the Exchange System at my first opportunity, so there is another package to look for. Again Kitten, I miss you something fierce. Steve.

May 11, 1968, Vietnam: There was a different tone in this letter from Steve. There was a big push in Vietnam, and the loss of men was definitely affecting him. He had spent many days flying Special Forces teams into hot areas.

Dear Brent, I am doing quite a bit of reconsidering about our plans for R&R. Japan seems to be going by the boards. Another thing Kitten, I want our bank account to have a steady amount at all times. Anyway, we have six or seven months to save funds.

By the way, do not count on starting our family then. I may not be like the person you knew. I like to dance, drink, and shop; if my last R&R is any indication. I have made very few promises to you Brent during the time we have known each other. I promise to do my upmost to insure that you, one day, see Bangkok. No doubt my vision is clouded by comparing it with Vietnam, but I am sure you will find it an interesting city. I will keep you posted on how things are going. Right now I am again the lowest man on the squadron's R&R list. Hang tight, and we will see how things work out. There will be more packages arriving soon for all of you. Some things I will purchase in Okinawa on my way home. Time to hit the rack. See you around. Steve.

May 14, 1968, Vietnam: Dear Brent, glad to hear that you were pleased with the jewelry. It really was both interesting and a lot of fun to shop for the stones. The price I paid is roughly one-third of the stateside price. I took my time and easily looked at a hundred gems for each one I finally bought. Incidentally, pearls are bought the same way. Only the gold bracelets and charms were bought as is. Everything else was unset. The reason why many of the settings are alike is once I found one I liked, I stuck with the winner. The settings are also special in that they are made special to my "demands." A lot of hard work went into selecting, bargaining, and finally closing the deal. The "black stone" is a black star sapphire. The aquamarine, a blue zircon, is your birth stone. Your pearls are real, cultured, but real. The uniform shape gives them away. The opal is the most expensive ring in this batch.

If you have been reading the news you know things have picked up here in the north. The fighting is real. The Marines would not leave their dead and wounded. They also know we would not leave them up the creek. You know there are a lot of "crazies" in the Green Machine. No doubt, we are number one. It takes a lot of pressure to make a real Marine, but once you are in, you get a lot of brothers really worth having. I get pissed every time I see a dead or wounded Marine. Someone has screwed with something very important to me. Hard to explain. Guess I never will be able to explain. We are definitely giving one hell of a lot more than we are receiving. See you around, Steve.

May 26, 1968, Vietnam: Dear Brent, Good afternoon Brent. Looks like this month will be one of my best flight months, despite seven days off for R&R.

Do not worry about R&R Brent. My next one is six months away, so save your money. Besides, this way we will not be saying good-bye for so long. Believe me, I will not go for leaving you again Brent after only five hectic R&R days. I can't really enjoy the world again in that length of time, to say nothing of getting use to you. People who play those games are fooling themselves. The wife does not understand the man that is supposed to be her husband, and he can't really enjoy her because he needs to get use to what is happening about him first. In other words, five days do not leave enough time to do anything. The guy comes back to Nam without having blown off steam and not having relaxed; he did not get used to being around his wife. He has shot an R&R all to hell. So relax, and we will do something when the first tour is about finished. Remember, I am also considering extending.

You are going to have a time getting me tamed again, Brent. I have gotten so old and so young at the same time. I really do not know what you will think. I know myself very well now. The "real you" shows up pretty quickly over here. All and all, I am very smug about the whole thing. I hope you will be happy about the change. Kind of a screwed up subject if I ever heard one!

I am sending you some pictures. Most were shot while we were aboard the Iwo Jima in the Tonkin gulf. These enlisted people are really outstanding. They fly all day, and work until all hours getting set to fly the next day. The rest of the pictures are just shots of the beach, etc. nothing special. My slide pictures are coming out excellently. I am shooting around twenty exposures a week. The prints are not the best, but they show a few scenes.

Thing are fine as I have said. Do you realize that more than half of my flight hours have been in combat. Definitely getting salty as hell. Steve.

June 8, 1968, Vietnam: Dear Brent, Good evening Darling! Good day for me and hope it was the same for you. We are still flying good long hours. Plenty of flight time and a lot of work done. I hope it hurts Charlie really bad.

Today I flew my HAC (Helicopter Air Commander) check and also got my section leaders check out of the way at the same time. Had two one wheel landing zones at around fifteen hundred feet. Both times the bird was loaded to the hilt. Made it with no sweat. Six hours later the check pilot said I had made the grade. Also said, I flew one of the best check rides he had given in quite a while. More importantly he said, "I had no visible problem areas."

What do you think of that!? I made HAC at around five hundred and fifty hours of flying, right at the squadron's lower time requirement. Next comes night carrier qualification from the right seat. Then it's "watch out world!"

The peace talks are getting to some of the other side. Captured N.V.A. personnel say they are pissed their government denies their presence in South Vietnam. They are proud of helping fight the United States and want their share of credit. I do not understand how we can have any kind of talks without defining a few terms.

The President's Unit Citation came through for our action in the fight for Khe Sanh. Only those who fought there are supposed to wear the ribbon. We lost nearly a bird a day there, and the squadron doesn't warrant the medal? About half the squadron's pilots and crews will get the award. Only one other lieutenant had more time than I up there, and he was a HAC.

Well Kitten, how is your job going? Say "Hi" to everyone. Steve.

June 10, 1968, Vietnam: Dear Brent, Good evening Darling. Things going well with you? Sure hope so! Things are going along fairly well here. Still flying a lot. Everything that hurts Charlie is well worth the sore butt.

Well, guess I have a claim to fame. I personally made the 70,000th landing on the U.S.S. Princeton. Even got my picture taken. I must confess I could not find the enthusiasm the sailors expected. Now they want me to cut some cake. All this while I could be doing something useful.

Got my night landing out of the way. Five right seat landings and by Navy regulations I can now fly off the carrier at night. Only have been doing just that right up until we found time to "qualify." Wasted time and unnecessary stress on aircraft and crews.

Made a few enemies in high places this evening. Had a cake cutting, picture taking deal for the 70,000[th] landing. The big deal was scheduled to go at 1300, however, the Navy forgot that the pilots would be flying over northern I Corps at that time. All the Navy aboard arrived, but no Marines. So it was put off until 1900. Who arrives at 1850 after being gone for eight hours over Khe Sanh and the DMZ, but yours truly. Ordered to the "big deal" by the X.O. I arrive only to learn that I was going to miss chow and shower hours for "your claim to being a hero" as one person put it. I told them that the Navy would have to cut its own cake as far as I was concerned. That caused a bit of concern, no one wanting to tell the ship's Captain the pilot who made the landing had told them to shove their sword and cake. So the HAC cut the cake and laughed at the Captain's jokes and kissed the Navy's ass. I walked out. When I have lost count of the dead and wounded I have carried back while here, I am supposed to be thrilled because a landing happens to be a round number. Do not worry, Brent. They will not do anything. I am a good damn Marine and a damn good pilot. I never signed anything saying I had to play games with the Navy. Take care, Steve.

June 25, 1968, Vietnam: Dear Brent, Good evening Darling. Hope things are going well for you and the rest of the tribe. This member of the tribe is doing well. The Ugly Angels are really going to town this month. It looks as if we will reach two thousand hours this month.

Personally I should easily break a hundred hours: a month well spent. Time passes extremely fast this way.

Well, glad to hear that you are so pleased with buying the house on the Blake Road. If the place is as represented, we should do alright. I think we shall operate under the "camp" idea. It gives us "roots" if we should ever need them, and we can fix it up a bit at a time. Besides, as a house it is not much, but as a camp it isn't bad. Besides, now we have some land!

The way the PUC for Khe Sanh works is that everyone that fought there gets the ribbon. The thing that bothers me is that our squadron had working birds there for one month. During this time our birds got badly shot up. We did not send inexperienced people to Khe Sanh and so just a few of us flew day after day up there. However, my point is that everyone busted their asses getting those shot up birds ready to go for tomorrow. In other words, I think everyone that was in the squadron at the time should get the award. It was a squadron effort. After a month we had lost so many birds we technically ceased to be a fighting unit and had to be pulled off the line. It did not really matter for Hue required our attention about this time. Anyway, it is my feeling that the Marines in maintenance gave a lot also during the fight for Khe Sanh.

Well, enough of the war stories. On to more pressing problems. Begin looking for another package. We have a couple of things coming from the Army and Air Force Exchange Service. I am also receiving the Meredith News alright. Tell Grampa and Grammie that I certainly appreciate them sending the paper. Steve.

The first six months of letters to Steve were not returned with his belongings. They may have been lost when his sleeping quarters were flooded when he was aboard ship.

N

June 30, 1968: Moultonborough, NH: Dearest Steve, Well, it has been a busy week for me. How were things for you? Tomorrow is July! I hope it flies!

I worked Saturday at the Clinic. About ten people from the Clinic staged a "robbery" of the old locomotive, with the governor aboard. This was, of course, for the Diamond Jubilee celebrations. The clinic people were all dressed up as robbers; a very funny sight. I didn't get to see the "robbery" as I had to work until 1:00 p.m. and the train came in at 12:30. The train will be here for rides during the celebration.

After work, I went to a friend's camp on Lake Ossipee for a long boat ride. I didn't realize how big that lake is. They had an adorable little puppy. She surprised me when she said her husband was thirty-nine years older than her.

Then, I rushed back home to catch the tail end of your Dad's birthday party. There was another puppy there. It was so cute I took it to my brother's for the children to enjoy.

I had been invited for a get together by a girl at work. I just called her and told her I couldn't make it. That would have been the last straw, as I was already exhausted. And, people ask me what I do in my spare time!

I hope we hear from the land survey on "our" place this week. I would like to start fixing it up a little.

Oh say, my boss will be back to work tomorrow. It will probably be dull now; since I got used to doing more with her gone. Although, the summer people will he here soon, and I shall be busy enough.

Will close for now, Honey. Hope to hear from you tomorrow. Take good care of yourself. I love you and miss you so very much. All my love, Brent.

July 5, 1968, Moultonborough NH: Dearest Steve, Hope you had a "nice" Fourth of July. I was really busy per usual. Wednesday night my mother, my brother's mother-in-law, and I went to the Wolfeboro fireworks.

By the way! You are now the proud uncle of an 8 pound 14 ounce baby boy named Donald James Cheney. He was born July 2 at 12:20 a.m. His mother is fine and so is he.

Yesterday, I had off work, so your dad and I met with the surveyor to walk the lines of our place. What a man the surveyor is. He has white hair, but he headed off through the woods like mad. I was panting to catch up!

 So, he determined that there are more than 800 feet on the pond! The exact acreage is yet to be figured, however, he thinks about 15 to 20 acres. It is a good hunk of land. It goes up to the school line. You will now own one of your favorite deer site hunting places, Honey! Your dad saw all sorts of deer signs.

The application for the money is going in and it is supposed to be all settled by July 15th. I was wondering if we could refinance this when you get home? It would take the mortgage off from your folk's place. Time will tell.

I am wondering what the next packages from you will be! The packages from Thailand have not arrived yet. So you plan to buy some more guns! You will not know which one to use—like me and my rings!

After seeing the property, I went to Tuftonboro for a neighborhood cookout. It was nice to see those people again. After the cookout, I took my mother, my brother's mother-in-law, and his children to Laconia to ride on the steam engine train that is there for the fourth of July celebration.

We had a good time on the train and saw a couple of the doctors and office people from the Clinic. The train went up to Meredith and back. We were, as promised, all covered with cinders by the end of the trip!

When I returned home I just missed your folks on the way to the Meredith fireworks.

I didn't know exactly where they stopped, so I went to Longwood for a late supper. Wondered how I found myself alone on the Fourth of July! So, I went over to Aunt Gertrude and Uncle Herbie's house. Herbie Jr. was there so we all talked for a while and I went home; even beat the folks home.

Sure wish you were here. Almost seven months now. Hope they keep rolling by fast. I miss you an awful lot.

We had paid $1,000.00 on the camp and land, you know. How does it feel to you to be at least $10,000 in debt? I think we have a good thing though, don't you?

It sounds as though you have been really busy, Honey. What are deaf mute heavies? You have used that term before, so what do you mean?

Will have to close for now Honey. I will put this in the mail and get back to work. I feel very ugly today for some reason. I just need my Steve something awful. He knows how to make Kitten purr and be nice. Take care of yourself Honey. I love you. Brent.

July 7, 1968, Moultonborough, NH: Dearest Steve, Sure do miss you Honey. Wish you were here to talk to me and to do things with.

After work Friday, I went home and then back to the Playhouse. I saw "Star Spangled Girl." It was a cute play but not very deep. It was fun to see the actors in person anyway. As it was a sudden decision on my part, no one was able to go with me.

Yesterday, your mother and I went down to see our new nephew, Donald James Cheney, and found out that he would not be home until today. We got to see the other children anyway.

Your folks bought a lobster and clam lunch to have on a canoe ride to the upper pond. They had a really good time. Also, your mother is working on our eagle rug again!

Soon I will start fixing up our camp! That will keep me busy. I want it all ready for you to come home to with all of our things in it. Most of all I want you in it.

Won't it be fun! You can put the stereo together, go out and hunt, and do all sorts of neat things. I am going to burst with joy just thinking about it and trying to contain myself until you are here.

Will close for now, Honey. Hope to hear from you again soon. Take care, I love you. Brent.

July 11, 1968, Vietnam: Dear Brent, Good evening! I hope this letter finds you in good shape. Everything is going well here for yours truly. Getting a lot of hours flying this month. Keeping busy anyway. I flew nine and three-tenths hours the Fourth of July. By the looks, this month will be another bear.

Saw my first OV-10A. Either those or Huey gunships are my next aircraft. Believe me, I am going to give Charlie some gray hairs. Once this squadron breaks up, I do not want to fly another aircraft with the same mission. My goals in this squadron are two hundred carrier landings, eight hundred combat missions and to never turn down a medevac. After that, I figure I owe Charlie another message from me to him. Besides, my personality fits the mission of an attack aircraft.

I have a card here announcing the arrival of Donald James Cheney. Please tell them that I am properly impressed and share a bit of their happiness. Your brother and his wife seem to be showing us their heels. I always was a bit slow on the uptake. Wonder what I am doing wrong?

I know despite the lack of money I enjoyed my tall, slim, and terrific young woman an awfully lot. We gained in one respect and lost in another, yet I think soon we will pretty much have our cake and eat it also.

Incidentally, the squadron is ashore again. The Navy has gone to Subic Bay for a rest. We off loaded in a day and then towed the mark bright and early the next day.

Well honey, I have been flying HAC lately. Been bringing them back pretty regular, so I thought it would be safe to crow a bit. Flying from the right seat is different, but I am learning slow but sure. I have even flown with my roommate. Most of the guys are very capable pilots. Flying night seat does keep one on his toes however.

Going through one of those times again, Honey. I need you all the time, Darling. I am sure you realize that; at times however, I have to tell you how much I miss you. It doesn't make things any easier to read about it. Being selfish like I am Kitten, I am sure I need you more than any man has needed any woman. I am not any man, and you are not any woman. I long to see you again and to bask in the warmth of our love. I want to hold you in my arms and love each other.

Enough! Be it known throughout the land that I miss my woman very deeply. I want her very much. Good night Kitten. Steve.

July 15, 1968, Moultonborough, NH: Dearest Steve. At lunch break the Clinic Manager saw me writing and asked me if I was writing my "boyfriend." I said: "Yes." I should have said "No," my husband. Actually I think he knew that.

I've realized this is a marriage by mail. Do you realize that by our third anniversary, we will have spent only half of the time together! Good grief !

My poor boss is down there typing like mad. There were about six camp children and several other "walk-ins" just as I left for lunch. She will be in a good mood when I get back after doing all of those charts! I offered, but she didn't want me to stay.

The loan has been approved for the "camp." We are still waiting for the survey. The payments will be every month for 20 years! I hope we are able to pay it off before then!

Oh say! We have a good refrigerator now. Your Dad sold a new one to a fellow, and said he could throw his old one out. Dad took it to "Martin's dump" and, I think it will serve us just fine for a while.

It is much better than the one in the camp. Your dad is sure doing well by us!

My deep fryer and your binoculars arrived Friday. Very nice indeed. I really wanted that deep fryer. Someone said you won't have anything left to get me for Christmas! I told them I just want you for Christmas. Yah! I'm going to attack you for sure!

Our "want list" is really getting a lot of attention. We sure are lucky. Actually, I haven't done too badly on my purchases.

Little Donald is doing well. He came home last week. Brother Wayne had his 26th birthday yesterday. I went down to the farm for the afternoon and evening.

We are sure glad you received your package from us. We will try to get another one sent off soon.

By the way, does Thailand smell the way the papers in the bronzeware box smelled? Your dad's Marine friend says the country smells that way and that you will too when you get home. Oh boy! We shall have to put you outside to air out, Honey!

Will close for now Dear. Take really good care of yourself. Sorry I can't tell you more about the camp at the moment. Hope to get a letter from you today. Love, Brent.

July 20,1968, Vietnam: Dear Brent, Things have slowed down a bit here, but I should get my hundred hours easily. Hours are not much to chase, but it is all time spent in the air, free of the ground.

Glad to hear that you have a new, white, one piece swim suit as well as a tan. I need you so much Kitten. I can never explain to you what you and your love have and will continue to mean to me.

It is really frightening to depend upon someone so whole heartedly. With every fiber of my being I love you Darling. My feeling of love for you is the purest, truest emotion I have within me. I promise you that your Marine will come home Brent, and when he does you may wish to continue the marriage "by mail."

I am really glad to hear about the loan coming through. Dad and Mom have certainly done much more than their share. We are very lucky, Kitten.

Glad to hear you are pleased with the bronzeware. Clean it as you would silver. It requires a bit of elbow grease and time. This particular style is quite rare and in two or three days of looking just for bronzeware, I did not see another like it. In fact there was only one set and other set was made to my order.

Since I began this letter, we have come back aboard the Princeton. It was nice to have received a short letter from your folks. Very nice, and I will return one as soon as time allows. Got to go! Steve.

July 23, 1968, Moultonborough, NH: Dearest Steve. It was certainly wonderful to receive your last letter. That's the kind I like to get. I like to know that you want me very much, as I want you. I can't imagine what it will be like when you get home. I know we have both changed considerably. You will never know, but it was really a traumatic experience when you left me to go to war. You can't imagine how much I depended upon you for everything.

I feel that I am more independent. I can be content within myself, as you are at times. I know that I will want to live every minute with you completely and fully. Live each day as my last because life has a way of getting by one. I feel as though I am an elastic band that is being stretched to its limit. Don't be surprised if I go all to pieces when I finally see you again. It will be the relief from twelve long months of tension. Enough of that or I'm going to start right now.

I must tell you about an interesting weekend. I went to Portland to visit Sue. While there, I met a Green Beret she had invited to dinner. He is a Major and has more ribbons and brass than I have ever seen. He has the Nation's highest award, plus some from other countries. He was a very interesting person to listen to. I know you are gritting your teeth, but I'm sure he must be one of the "better" Army products. I told him only second best!

Did you ever hear of a Lieutenant's wife telling a Major he was only second best? He deserved it: telling me Green Berets are better than Marines. I have news for Him! So, watch out if you ever see Major "Smith." You tell the Navy off and I'll tell a few majors where to get off. It is fun to spar a little now and then. By the way, he was at the siege of Khe Sanh. You may have worked together. It was good luck to see someone from where you are, and it was all in good jest. He also praised the Marine helicopter crews.

Say, your carvings have arrived. Are they ever beautiful! They are over the fireplace at your folks with your sword. They are really very beautifully done.

You know the land and everything is held up because of the survey. By the time you get home it may be settled! It is discouraging. I'm glad I haven't really done any work on it or really claimed it yet. It is taking so long for the wheels of progress to turn.

You know Steve, I am very proud of you. I'm glad you are flying HAC. I trust your judgement more than anyone else's. I know you are doing a good job. The men are lucky that get to fly with you. I know that if anyone knows what they are doing, it is you. The Major said a reason he is going back is that there are so many people over there who don't know what they are doing. He feels his experience is needed. I don't know what to say when you want to change your mission. I sure have a tiger by the tail with you. How will I ever keep you tied down now? Would children keep you home for a while, Honey?

Good night for now my husband. I need you desperately. Love, Brent.

August 4, 1968, Moultonborough, NH: Dearest Steve, Your little wife has been running herself ragged. I think I am tired; as I have never been so busy in my life!

So how does it feel to be a land owner, Honey? You have 20 acres of land with a1,400 foot access to the pond, a two bedroom house, cottage, or camp: whatever you want to call it!

I hope you are still pleased about all of this, Honey. I feel we have something now! It's really a lot of fun. The best will be when you come home, and we go to the bank to have it signed over to you (us)!

Your dad has mowed the lawn, and Grampa Martin has started on the bushes. I couldn't believe it but before we know it, we will have a view of the pond. Everyone likes the camp now that they have been inside it—even Grammie Martin! Dad has the water running and the lights are on. I am looking at wall paper and paint, etc.

I worked Friday night and Saturday which are overtime hours. People are on vacation so this will be for three weekends. We sure can use the money!

So, you are a man of the world now, and I think I am going to like you this way. Being basically a sound person, I guess I can take it. I'm really going to learn to dance now. Tonight your mother and dad took me to Meredith for pizza and beer. Being Sunday, they wouldn't serve us beer! So, we had pizza and coffee. Anyway, the place has a beautiful view.

We are sending you more underwear. What do people wear over there? Why can't you buy underwear? You can get everything else, but underwear!

My brother tipped his big tractor over the other day. He didn't get hurt, thank goodness. I guess anyone can do that as they are not foolproof at all! Anyway, he likes our place and has offered to help me out with it.

We saw three ducks and also deer tracks on our land today, Honey. Pretty good, huh! I can't wait for you to come home. It will be so wonderful. I sure do miss you. Good night. I love you, Brent.

August 9, 1968, Moultonborough, NH: Dearest Steve, So how goes the battle? Here I am working another long Friday night.

I bought a can of ceiling paint for the camp. One room needs attention immediately. I am really looking for wallpaper. Once I do one room it will snowball on me; as then, the others won't look so great. There is a lot to be done on the place, if one so wishes. The major decisions will have to be made by you though, such as where the bathroom will be enlarged!

Sure hope I hear from you again soon. I sure do miss you Steve. I'll be so glad when you come home to me again. It is much too long to be separated.

In our camp I think I like our living room best. It is about 11 feet by 17 feet. The bedrooms and kitchen are about 11 by 11 feet.

Grampa Martin has really done a lot of work outside, mowing and raking the lawn, etc. He will have us that view before we know it!

I guess I will have to finish this letter later. Patients are coming in for evening office hours.

Hi! At work we were really busy over the weekend, with Saturday being the busiest ever.

Today I picked up my parents to see our house, and they liked it. I then took them out to lunch. I don't think I remember ever having a meal in a restaurant with my father. Mom yes, but not him. He was very nice and flirted with the waitresses. He really liked those miniskirts, and I really did have a good time with them.

Will close for now, Honey. Take good care of yourself. I miss you terribly. It is almost impossible to bear at times. I love you Steve. Please hurry home. Love, your Kitten.

August 10, 1968, Vietnam: Dear Brent, Greetings Darling: Good evening and I hope everyone is in fine shape. Things are going along just fine here. Looks like another good month. What a bear!

Excuse my using the back of these thin pages, but I have run out of money and stationary at the same time. Seems they have decided to pay me what I am worth, not what I am supposed to get. As of yet, I have not had a chance to go see the proper people about the whole thing. Seems strange to have one's pay drop off when you get a pay raise and finally make your last "dead horse" payment.

I am very glad to hear that you think the camp has possibilities. While it is not the house on the hill, it is a big step in the right direction. If you are there Kitten, I am quite sure that in the far distant future, I shall remember the camp with a good deal of warmth. My home is where you and my work are. Hope your work is going well. It sounds as if it keeps you busy. It also serves to get you out and doing things. Steve.

August 15, 1968, Moultonborough, NH: Dearest Steve. It was sure great to receive a letter from you today. It was quite a lapse before hearing from you again. Honey, I love you so very much.

So guess what! Your wife got a raise! Only five months of work and I got a raise. I didn't expect it until September! What a surprise when your friend Peter Miner and his bride walked into the Clinic. It so happened I found out about my raise with them standing there; plus I was trying to give someone directions on the phone. My boss handed me the check and as she pointed to the amount she said: "It will be this amount from now on." It took a second to sink in. Was I ever surprised; just about blew my "professional" cool to bits on that one!

Tonight Richard Wakefield came down to see our camp. He liked it a lot and has all sorts of plans for it; even as to where he will build our fireplace! He also helped me clean the car.

Your mother is off to Massachusetts to go on a rug exhibit tour, and you dad is starting his course for work. Now I'm alone and scribbling a few lines to you. I can't spell tonight either! Would you believe I've actually stayed home one evening.

The stereo sounds unbelievable. How can one possibly put that much into it? Is it all gold? I'm glad you are having a good time planning for it, Honey.

Funny thing about your pay. Wonder what the problem was. If you were paid what you are worth to me; they would not have enough money in the world, Honey.

So, will close for now and try to get to bed earlier tonight. We plan to go to Portland to the art show Saturday. Should be fun. Remember I love you and need you. We are going to have an unbelievable third Honeymoon! Love, Kitten.

August 19, 1968, Vietnam: Dear Brent, Well, down to business. This is what I would like you to do. I fully realize that your pay is your own so these ideas are just that—ideas. Make up your own mind on this as you are the portion of this partnership "on the scene" and have as much common sense as the other portion. I realize you may believe that I am spending money like a drunken sailor, but that is not the case.

Brent reads his financial plan! Is my argument logical to you? It is to me! So you had better do it! Seriously Kitten, I have to have enough money to wine, dine, and dance my way into a particular woman's arms. You see, after Vietnam, I would freeze to death on those cold, windy New England nights, and I will need someone to keep me warm.

I am sure we will be able to do a lot of fixing up the camp during my leave. I have even sent for a home furnishing catalog. Have to hit the rack. Love you Kitten. Steve.

August 20, 1968, Moultonborough, NH: Dearest Steve, So glad to hear from you twice this week! It sounds as though you are really busy. Speaking of buying things: I bought a sweater and a light jacket yesterday. You know I tore my old suede jacket "walking the lines" on our property.

Tomorrow night I am taking my brother, his wife, and my mother to the Play House to see Showboat. It should be nice, and I will let you know how it goes.

So you saw the Commandant. What was his mission with you? Phasing out 34's?

We are working on the ninth month now, Honey. Hope they fly by. Have to get through fall, and then you will be here!

I haven't done much on the camp yet. Just waiting for the finances to even out. The survey bill hasn't come yet. There is always a place for money!

You know when you get home you will need some new clothes. Plan on a shopping spree. Your civilian wardrobe is really at its lowest. It will be fun to shop together again, won't it. I am going to savor every minute of it.

I sure do miss you, Honey. It doesn't seem possible we have been apart for so long. A year is an unbelievable length of time to be apart. Together it was heaven, but now it seems like a unique torture. Did you ever feel like a time bomb? Just all set to go off and just ticking the time away.

I will cut this off and go down and visit with the grandparents. There is not much going on around town, so I will be sticking close to home. I don't know what I do with my time, it just sort of goes by. Good night, Honey. I love you and miss you so very much. Take care now. Your Brent.

August 22, 1968, Vietnam: Dear Brent, Good evening Honey! Good show on your raise. I am sure you have earned it. Things are busy here as we are flying every day.

Right now it sounds as if the Martin tribe is really spread out all over New England.

Everyone sounds busy and moving ahead with your various interests. Damn, I am proud of each and every one of you people. Always growing as individuals, yet still a tight family group. It really means a lot to be a Martin. I have got to get busy here. There are a lot more steps to climb.

Darling, I have got to go to bed and get some rest now. Kind of wish you were waiting there for me. Our third honeymoon is really going to be something. We are going to disappear behind our own closed doors, for about three days, and only come out for food and drink. Anyway, I sure talk big, huh? Steve.

August 25, 1968, Moultonborough, NH Dearest Steve, Summer is just about over. Labor Day is just around the corner. It did go fast in spite of myself. Keeping busy is the key. Work hard, play hard, and there will never be a dull moment—right?

I love you Mr. Martin, very much. I hope you realize how much your wife wants and needs you. I plan to convince you to never want to leave home again. I may have to use a little witchcraft, but you won't get away so easily next time. I protest. A husband and wife should be together. Maybe you should beat me now and then! It wouldn't bother me as much to have you away! Plan to see a lot of action on the home front, old warrior. Wining, dining, and dancing sound just about more than I can resist. I bet "this lady" will really fall for that line of yours.

Will close for now my love. Take good care of yourself. I love and miss you desperately. Love, Kitten.

August 25, 1968, Vietnam: Dear Brent. Good evening Darling. How is the battle going? Everything and everyone is okay here.

The UH-34D is not going to be phased out at all. Because of the job we have been doing, the 34's are to become part of the new HML Squadrons in country. In other words, 34's and Huey's will be all in one package. A really decent medevac package all neatly wrapped up just waiting to be utilized.

Since I had today off and nothing really pressing to do, I made up a tape with you in mind. There are around two solid hours of love songs. I must confess that my intentions are highly dishonorable. It is all part of my campaign to work my way back into your heart, Darling.

Brent, you haunt me! As I sit here listening to these songs I think of you and the warmth we share. No other woman could ever command the depth of emotion I have for you Darling. All the things these songs say, I feel so strongly for you. I want to return home and win you again; court you in a way no other woman has ever been: and so, the very special tape, Brent. After the dinner and dancing I am going to try to seduce you. Every wife needs this to boast her pride in herself and in her marriage. I need you Kitten. Please share the rest of what life has to offer with me. I want to keep things simple between us. Love, trust, and respect for each other only, as long as we shall live. I am packing a box of stuff I do not care to cart around any longer. Dad's watch will be among the goodies. Love, Steve.

September 1, 1968, Moultonborough, NH: Dearest Steve, Did you notice the last postmark? Yes, your wife was in Kalamazoo, Michigan. I was really "coerced" to drive out there to help take a friend and her car back to college. We left Friday night at six, after I got out of work. We arrived there at two p.m. Sunday afternoon. We took turns driving two hour shifts. The first stay was in Troy, New York. The next night was in Toledo, Ohio. We almost didn't get a room the last night. We ended up in a motel's lecture room on roll away cots! That was better than sleeping in the car.

I should now be more help to you on our little jaunts. I got some turnpike driving experience and got us through Troy, New York. The four lane traffic in Cleveland, Ohio was interesting. We even got a glimpse of lake Erie.

The mid-west is quite flat as expected, and the soil is very black. The city of Kalamazoo is very clean and pretty. The college campus is really nice. There are a lot of new buildings, and they are real architectural wonders. The girls have a very nice apartment.

I couldn't wait for the flight back home. As you know this was my first flight! It was a great trip and I am so glad I went. It was a last minute decision, and I was lucky to get a plane reservation to get back home. I had to be back to work Tuesday. Nothing like taking off for a weekend!

Good night Honey. Please take good care of yourself, Steve. I love and miss you very much. Only four more months to go. Hold on! Love, your Brent.

September 4, 1968, Moultonborough, NH: Dearest Steve, You have done so well with your purchases. I feel giddy with all of this really happening to us. Every dream I have ever dreamed has come true since we have been married, Steve. I am so afraid someone is going to "burst my balloon," that I tread softly and carry a big club.

I can be with a roomful of people, including your folks who are number one with me, and still be alone for the need of your presence. You will never know how much I need you in my life. Your very presence will fill this house with all the warmth that has been missing for so many months. This whole family revolves around you Steve. Hurry home!

I know I have changed as you said. I'm probably not the same person you left. I expect that you are not either. However, I know we could not have gone through a year like this without it affecting us. I feel that we have changed much in the same way. I think we are tougher; that we both want to savor every bit of life and living that we can. We will never stand still Honey.

I must say this new radio is tremendous. I have it on F.M. and it is so nice to listen to. The tonal quality is unbelievable. Thanks a lot, Honey!

By the way, I think flying is tremendous! Everyone should do it at least once. What a world, all its own up there. It makes the world look so small and all its troubles look so petty. It seemed like I was in a dream. The pressure in the plane bothered my head a little; like I had one drink too many! It was fun to fly first class and to have a steak dinner! I didn't get a cocktail—only coffee.

It was so fantastic to have taken two days to get to Michigan and to be back in less than two hours! What an experience! I love it! There was a lightning storm too, and I even liked that. The flight took off in daylight and landed on the east coast in the dark. Really great. It was an ultra-tremendous weekend.

I have been looking at some courses I might take. Although my mind will not be very attentive for the next four months. I'm hopping out of my skin for December to get here for your return. I'm going to use every "wile" in my power to get you under my spell again: steak dinners, your favorite liquor, soft music, low light, perfume, sexy clothes, etc. What do you say? I say I love you Sir! Will close for now my love. Take good care of yourself. Love, Kitten.

September 1968 Moultonborough, NH: Dearest Steve, Must say I am very proud of you "Captain" Martin! Congratulations! Now you have to tell me all of the details. When effective and all that. I can hardly believe it. You are a young Captain! The only thing I regret is that I am unable to pin those double bars on you. The first ones I have missed. I'm really going to have to shape up now. I'm really going to have to wait now for "audiences" to see you. To celebrate, we all went out to dinner. Love, Brent.

N

Several letters went back and forth between Steve and Brent dwelling mostly on spending, budgets, and the usual messages of concern and love.

N

September 15, 1968, Moultonborough, NH: A letter from Mother Martin, My Dearest Son. Well, how is the old world treating you? Everything is fine here. It's really beginning to look like fall, and we have had some glorious days. Do you realize next week we start the tenth month you have been gone! Great!

Brent wanted me to tell you she will write as soon as she can stay awake long enough. Don't worry as she is o.k. She is curled up on the couch with Peanuts the kitten. The doctor said she has a touch of mono. Another family member had similar symptoms but recovered quicker.

You will be pleased to know that Brent got a package from you containing some lovely records. Some friends were visiting and were just overwhelmed with all the lovely things you have sent home. They thought Brent was really lucky and much loved. Take good care of the best son ever. All my prayers. Love, Mom.

Dear Son, How are things going with you? I am bearing up pretty well considering I have three women to put up with. Bear hunting has opened up, and they have shot a few up north.

Your radio that you sent home sure is a honey. Brent had it fixed up and it works really well. When you get home, your house should be well wired with your radio, stereo and all the rest. Well, have to go to work now, so take care and we will see you. Love, Dad.

N

September 25, 1968, Vietnam: Dear Brent, Good evening Darling. Well, are you feeling any better? I hope things have smoothed out a bit for you. Things are fine here, and there is really not much going on.

Well Brent, we have received our orders for our next duty station. Seems that we will be returning to the training command. Just where in the command, I can't say; but most likely, somewhere in the Florida complex. Well, what do you think of that? I do not think it is really that bad.

So get ready to ship our stuff again. This time around Kitten, we shall do quite a bit more. In fact, I have actually too many irons in the fire. You probably have more than just a couple yourself.

I want to get my F.A.A ratings for fixed wing and helicopters, as well as instrument ratings for both. A multi-engine rating would not be that bad either. Then, I want to get checked out in a couple of other birds. I also want to start taking some extension courses, as many as possible that will help me toward my Master's Degree. I would like to start some serious target shooting too. Think I will get half of it done?

Once I am home, we shall sit down to a "summit meeting." Taking pencil in hand and giving voice to our thoughts, we will thrash out a Martin five year plan.

Received some good news today. The squadron is allowing us to go on shopping trips to Hong Kong, Japan, and Okinawa, etc. I would like to get one to Hong Kong and get some more things I have been wanting. Well, Kitten, enough is enough. Steve.

September 26, 1968, Moultonborough, NH: Dearest Steve, I received a letter from an interesting young man about his mortgage. I believe you overstated the amount?

Actually Honey, I haven't done that badly. We have more in savings than when you left. So there! I must admit I haven't been as frugal as I could have been. I've spent money on just plain going places.

Your budget looks good Honey, except one area. The food budget, I'm afraid we shall find, needs an increase. Prices have risen considerably since we were keeping house. This is an area, for which, we shall have to make allowances. I expect to have a full larder with which to tempt my man. I've been looking at our things and can't wait to use that deep fryer. Oh boy! I'm really getting excited about getting you home and setting up housekeeping again!

According to your Dad's course, one is a "household executive;" not just a housewife! So, I plan to become a "household executive" again soon.

I am reading your book, "Those Who Love." I always did like historical novels.

When is you due date home? Is it in December or January? I'd hate to be working when you get home. Will end for now, Honey. Remember, I love you very much and am looking forward to your return. Love, Brent.

October 1, 1968, Moultonborough, NH: Dearest Steve. Three years ago tonight we were rehearsing for the "big event." It is hard to believe the time has passed so quickly. Sure wish you were here to celebrate with me, Honey. How does one celebrate a wedding anniversary without one's husband? You just don't, I guess. We really have some catching up to do!

So, it looks like Florida again! I'm not really too surprised. I'm trying to think where would be a good place to look for our quarters. I suppose it depends on which field you are connected with. I assume you will be an instructor. That is the idea, isn't it?

About the mono: older people never get it. It occurs usually in teens through people in their early twenties. A neighbor said her son had it at three years of age. Another lady said she had it when she got married. Doctors don't know how it is communicated (1968). Of course it is known as the "kissing disease" which is embarrassing. I always thought it was odd as most of the kids in school who ever got it were the most unlikely in that aspect. People with a good immune system don't get as sick as I did. If it is only the worst ailment I ever get, I shall consider myself lucky. Guess I have felt sorry for myself long enough.

You certainly have an ambitious program outlined for yourself. It sounds like a busy life, Honey. I'm certainly looking forward to that "summit talk." I am looking forward to the life ahead also, Steve. We must cherish every minute that we have together, Honey. I love you Steve and miss you more than you can imagine.

Do you think you will be able to do our Christmas shopping in Hong Kong? Let me know how you do, and I'll fill in on this end.

Will close for now, Honey. I will look forward to your next letter. I love you and miss you. Please hurry home. Tell me what you did on our anniversary! My folks gave us a lovely card for our anniversary. They wanted you to know. Love, Your Brent.

October 1, 1968, Vietnam: Dear Brent, Good evening Darling. How are things with you? Things are fine here although I am not flying that much.

Well Darling, in another ten minutes it will be our third anniversary. It has been three wonderful years for me Darling. They seem really short to me. I wonder where we will be and where we shall stand in only twenty or so years. I am sure happiness shall continue to be ours.

I am very glad to hear that the china sets have begun to arrive. Keep watching! There should be a few gasps, etc. I hope you are pleased and that the china wears well. Is it what you wanted?

You take it easier from now on. I have enough plans to wear you out when I get home.

I think we should be able to swing the increase in the food budget. No sweat. We will bend the assets to fit our needs.

I may have a chance to go to Hong Kong on a four day shopping trip pretty soon. I may be able to get a few things for the tribe's Christmas.

I really think it is about time we had a kid. Not necessarily because of your reasons, but to fulfill our love in many ways. Besides, some people are beginning to doubt my manhood. How about a son the first time around? I would really like a son to grow up with.

I see HHH is selling us down the drain. A halt in bombing will mean more young American men will die. I have not been wrong that often, if you remember some of my other "feelings" on things over here. Charlie will use a halt to strengthen his position. Either sooner or later it will cost us big. Things just do not happen the way John Wayne presents things in "Green Beret." The sooner people realize war is serious and so very human. Somehow, I think war shows man at his stupidest and at his best. I suppose you can't actually see it, but for a man to conquer fear is a glorious thing.

Well Kitten, what do you think of my many plans? Which ones do you think warrant serious attention? What are your irons you desire on the fire? Take it easy. Steve.

This is the last letter from Steve to Brent.

October 9, 1968, Vietnam: Good evening Brent, How are things going with you? Things are pretty busy right now thanks to my flying a L.M.D. (Large Metal Desk). Still not flying that much, but now the Colonel knows my name my spare time is all planned for me. I am, and will continue to fly every chance I get. By the way, I am now a test pilot for the UH-34. According to the awards section I now have 47 air medals. So I am well on the way towards my 1,000 missions.

I am sorry to say that I had to turn down my first medevac two days ago. One good thing was that the Marine was not very badly hurt. If he had been an emergency, I believe I would have gotten him out. However, I would have damaged the bird to do it.

They were Recon Marines and they had no real zone; just a hole to drop the hoist through the canopy of the 75 feet to the deck. They were on a steep mountain side about a thousand feet above sea level and completely out of the wind. I tried three times and was unable to hover well enough to pick the poor guy up. He would have pulled me down rather than me pulling him up. This was the first one I have ever told that I could not hack it. I hope I never have to tell anyone else I can't get to them. It really burns me! We do not leave medevacs out in the field.

The people down here are back in the battle. Three days ago we began an operation to clear the area surrounding Thuong Duc Special Forces Camp. Mixing it up like up North. These guys are Marines.

I do not think I will go to Hong Kong this month. I have figured I need to save a little more before I go.

Girlie, you are going to have such a "make" thrown on you. Stand by! Quality may not be much, but quantity (in my mind only) will be something. Do you feel as I do Kitten? What I am really looking forward to is getting to know you again and losing myself in the "us" once again. If it was not for you Brent, I could easily stay over here for I am a very highly motivated Marine. There are a great many important persons, ideas, and ideals in my life. You are the most important Kitten, for in you I found my ideal of love, womanhood, and marriage. I am realistic enough to know ideals are not found very often in this very human, and therefore gray world of ours. I know that this man has been very happy for the last three years, and this guy believes firmly in romantic love, and is sure he and his wife share it.

How much longer do you think our car will last? A clean, working car fulfills my requirements for transportation. What are your thoughts? Take care Darling. Steve.

THIS IS THE LAST LETTER TO CAPTAIN STEVEN W. MARTIN, HMM 362, F.P.O.S SAN FRANCISCO, CALIFORNIA 96602, FROM BRENT. It came back stamped: RETURNED TO WRITER, U.S. MARINE CORPS REPORTS UNDELIVERABLE.

October 8, 1968, Moultonborough NH: Dearest Steve, Thank you so much for the lovely roses. You can't imagine how happy I was to receive them. I took one of them to work and everyone thought it was nice. The patients coming in exclaimed over it, and I was really happy. Happy, because it was mine and that you had sent it to me.

Sunday, my brother helped me move our things to the camp. Honey, we have a bed and a mattress from my parents. Your dad is going to get the gas stove hooked up.

We will have to sleep up there and take possession of the place. Your plans for the future sound really fine. Glad to hear we are saving so well for the future.

My mother is really not very well. Saturday, I stayed there overnight. She is lucky to have Wayne and his family there. Your mother is busy with her classes. She is a very active person.

Honey, did you ever receive a package from us over a month ago? We have just sent another one to you. Also, I guess we won't send a Christmas package. Do you think you will be home for Christmas? I sure hope so. We will save it for you. No Christmas until you are home! Good night Honey. Take care of yourself. I love you. Brent.

Note: The rose Brent took to work flourished and lasted for several days. The rest of the bouquet that was left at home faded and dried up quickly.

Journal: Days In The Life Of A Pilot

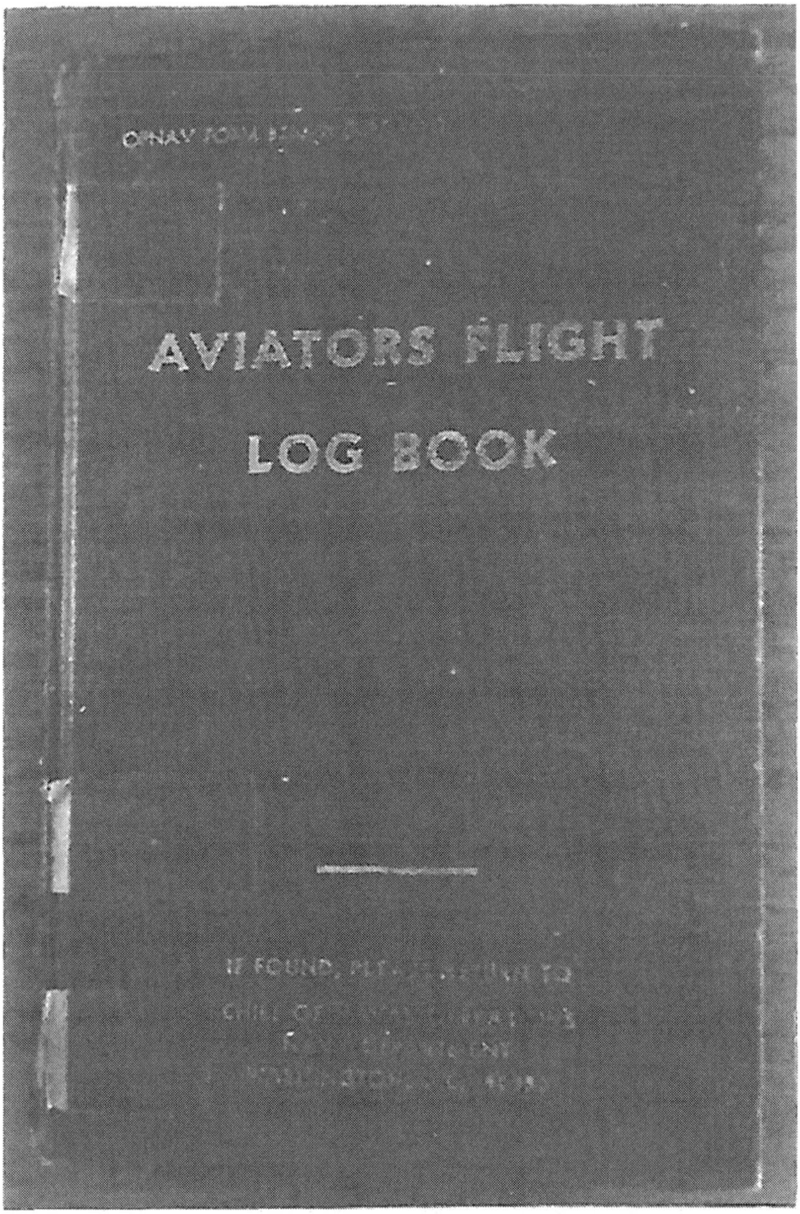

Chapter 8

The Journal

DAYS IN THE LIFE OF A UNITED STATES
MAINE CORP PILOT, 1968 VIETNAM
(Earlier journal entries, if any, were not with these.)

June 14, 1968: Flew 6.3 hours for the 9th Marines. We made four trips into their zone before we managed to get the medevacs out. A0-2 had their guns spotted, and by calling their shots gave us about 15 seconds to get out of the zone. The first three times they got rounds on us before we could get the medevacs aboard. The fourth try we got them aboard and got out. Went into A-4 and A-3 twice today and did not draw fire, not a usual event for a spiral approach.

June 15, 1968: Flew 4.7 hours C&C for the 3rd Marines.

June 16, 1968: Had SDO (Squadron Duty Officer) today. Another pilot had the squadron's fourteenth engine failure. Had four passengers at the time. Lost it at 50 feet and 40 knots. Hit hard in a paddy, gear was broken off, and the tail cut off the blades. Everyone got out alright.

June 17, 1968: SDO today. Night medevac is standing by on the Dubuque tonight. The Princeton is heading out to sea tonight. Afraid of an air attack tonight, and tomorrow we will take on supplies. (He was flying off the Princeton.)

June 18, 1968: Flew 6.0 hours today, C&C for the 9th Marines in the morning, and the Danang mail run in the afternoon. Perfect boredom!

Another pilot took seven hits from a .50 cal. coming out of a hill. We got a briefing tonight of plans that will be supported by helicopters. It could be tough during the monsoon. It all points to the North Vietnamese going all out for victory in 1968.

When Charlie could not overrun us, he did manage to outflank us. A good point to remember. The road was there for at least a month, just ten thousand meters south of Khe Sanh, before it was spotted. It is one of the most heavily flown over areas in Vietnam and all this was going on under our noses. Air power supports the grunts, it is not an end in itself. But for the grunts we would never have known they were there until they shot at us. I have flown over the road myself and didn't suspect a thing. The road is protected by antiaircraft emplacements. These are the underdogs people like to root for. Our women and children victims!

June 19, 1968: Flew 6.7 hours on Danang Mail Run. Pretty poor way to spend the day. Some of the ships were hit with missiles.

June 20,1968: Had night medevac and stood by in the Ready room all night. An area was hit this afternoon about 1600. The fire and explosions were clearly visible twenty miles away. Another area was completely closed down. The fires still going strong at 0600 the 21st when I went off duty. God help those there. One village after another disappearing in columns of smoke and debris.

The Princeton got its first real taste of Vietnam today. At about 1430 we took three explosions off to the starboard, five hundred to a thousand yards away. I wish I could count all the artillery, etc. I have taken within a half mile. We feel the round has to fall within two hundred yards to be sure they are shooting at you. Most fall within fifty yards easily. At times we took all kinds of artillery every time we touched down. After eight hours of flying, the whole thing got awfully old.

June 21, 1968: Day off. Boy, what a wasted day. Did not even eat today. Caught up on my sleep, at least. Damn this sitting on my ass. Have not done anything for the last two days.

Heard today that Brent put down $1,000.00 on the camp on Blake Road. I wish she had borrowed the money from Dad. That way I would repay him from the 10% savings when I return home. We would then have the maximum amount drawing interest in the two savings accounts. Besides having a goodly amount of money available in the bank would be handy if I get zapped.

Brent really provides my strongest anchor in the world. I have forgotten so much about her and our life together, but I can never forget the warmth we shared. Love is such a fragile thing, and yet, in some very lucky people's lives it is the strongest thing they know. I do not know what really makes me want to stay here and fight. Maybe it is because I am of use and can help. Maybe it is because I cannot sit back and allow others to fight my battles for me. Brent, nevertheless, provides my foundation in the world where people do not die violent deaths and live to kill before you yourself are slain. She is reason to look forward to surviving.

In many ways I and those like me, are no longer fit to return to the world. No longer do I believe in our leaders. They have sent our young men to rot in the corruption of war. Playing their parlor games with young men's lives. They then sold us down the river at Paris. Why!!!

June 22, 1968: Flew 5.6 hours. C&C with the 4th Marines and flew the investigators around the ammo dumps. They were trying to decide what caused the fires, rocket or artillery fire. It was the second time the dumps had been hit. God, if we are not careful we could lose a lot of men in this operation. We are bringing the runway with us. So much has to come out of that winding dirt road. Two battalions have taken to the mountains on either side to secure the route of march.

Some would write off any equipment not easily transportable. Not the Marine Corps, we are removing everything and going out by road, an extremely dangerous operation for a regiment in contact with two known enemy divisions. We need the men for the coming enemy thrust. Charlie will get his ass whipped once again.

The Princeton is getting ready for her own taste of war. It is believed the enemy may have been moving missiles closer. Understand they are quite good, could be interesting.

June 23, 1968: Flew 6.3 hours C&C for the 4th Marines. Saw my first big enemy convoy coming out a route. It was moving very slowly, feeling the way. Had two friendly artillery rounds pass close enough to really rock the aircraft today.

June 24, 1968: Flew 5.8 hours in country medivac. There are to be fire bases for the roving battalion. They are to be supplied by helicopter. It will be a different job during the monsoon; it is too damn high up. Think the big push will come in July/August. Plans seem to be to draw our troops away from the cities and then take and occupy one or more. Just another example of the Reds using the two sharp edges of revolutionary war.

June 25, 1968: Flew 4.4 hours C&C for the 4th Marines. The Brass had a few words for us tonight. Seems the big wigs ashore think we are skating out here on the boat. Have to put out more than ever before. I am afraid the birds will not stand up. Had ASE trouble with the first bird this morning. At high power settings the bird became almost uncontrollable. No radio communication between aircraft on F.M. per usual. An example of poor planning with two types of radios in the same squadron. Just can't talk between aircraft having two different types of F.M. Two birds with the new F.M. usually have no communication either. We should not fly in-country without communication between aircraft on the ground. Just isn't safe! I should be fairly close to going over a hundred hours for this month. Nearly twice the recommended combat load.

June 26, 1968: Flew 5.2 hours C&C for Dong Ha DASC. Took my 23rd hit today. Small arms round hit the step. Did not realized we were even shot at. Area gook incoming mortars while we were refueling. Went into A-3, conducted three U.R.'s and carried medevacs to the Repose from "D" Med. Bird was down with a hard-over in roll channel. A beautiful day.

June 27, 1968: Flew 2.7 hours on the mail run. Was flying the right seat, had no problems; taxiing needs a bit of work. Picked up seven PAX and 450 lbs. of mail out of LZ11. Not bad at all; took two tries however. Got four hours of sleep this afternoon. Another beautiful day; just a bit of heat haze. No F.M. communication between birds again today.

June 28, 1968: No fly. Day off. What I did not need. What a boring day. The Princeton thought they had a fire this evening. Another short in their alarm system. The two million dollars of air conditioning blows hot air a good bit of the time. Must say the Iwo Jima was a more reliable ship than some others.

June 29, 1968: Flew 4.3 hours. Had a Danang run and night medevac. One of our birds went down on the beach. It had a complete electrical failure and the battery blew up. In getting the battery overboard some acid splashed on the faces of a Captain and a Sergeant. They had picked up two medevacs. Another bird took the medevacs out. Our bird was loaded with mail, two other helicopters were loaded so we could not lift everyone out. Two machine guns were set up just at the sands edge, and we orbited above keeping an eye on things. An ARVN unit sent troops to secure the area and that is when our worse moment arrived. We landed just in time to stop those on the deck from cutting the ARVN's down. A new battery was flown in and the downed bird returned. Not a bad day. No hits, no runs, no errors.

June 30, 1968: Flew 4.3 hours C&C for the 4th Marines. Flew right seat; not a particularly good day.

Two birds downed with ASE problems. The first one had a hard-over just as I was lifting off with six pax. Bad radios also. The second had a kick in the roll channel.

July 1, 1968: Flew 7.0 hours C&C for the 3rd Marines. A lot of activity. Took heavy small arms and .50 caliber fire. The deck is all chewed up. Bad radio communication again today. One of our birds crashed and burned today on takeoff from the landing zone. The wind shifted 180 degrees and he lost his turns and settled into the trees. Crew and two pax made it out all right.

July 2, 1968: Flew 6.2 hours C&C for the 3rd Marines. Terrific winds today. Somewhere around 40 knots. Awfully easy to bust your ass. The 0.7 was a medevac pickup. "P" drew fire for his second time while he has been over here. He has taken only one hit. Not bad for 6 months in country.

July 3, 1968: Flew 5.8 hours C&C. Flew over most of northern I Corps. Went into Hill 950 on a beer run. People up there looked in rough shape. Landed aboard the St. Paul. Quite an experience! Activity along the DMZ pretty heavy.

July 4, 1968: Flew 9.3 hours. C&C and in-country medevac. Drew mortar fire while on the runway. The round landed in a Marine work party. Four were seriously injured. A General came aboard ship to present decorations. Twenty persons received decorations (four officers). Launched a medevac this evening. Drew fire on our way back. Poor radios all day.

July 5, 1968: Flew 6.4 hours C&C and medevac. Took five rounds of mortar fire. The landing zone was really piss poor. Wind currents beat you back and forth constantly. It is definitely more difficult to get off. Have my first HAC hop tomorrow.

July 6, 1968: Flew 6.6 hours C&C for the 3rd Marines. It seems as if nearly everyone had contact today. Area was taking incoming off and on all day. First mission of day was a medevac pickup. Saw a Doris Day flick tonight. Nice to see something with happy undertones. Everything always works out in the end just right. The hero gets the girl and girl gets hero.

July 7, 1968: Flew 4.0 hours. C&C for the 9th Marines. Lead got mortared both times into landing area. Poor radios again today. "R" jerked my chain at APM about "L" breaking a tail wheel locking pin.

July 8, 1968: Flew 5.9 hours. 2.1 hours were with Captain "C." bringing a tail section back to the ship. 3.8 hours were spent ferrying fresh bread, oranges, etc. to company positions. Lt. "S" was my copilot. We took 300 lbs. into an area. No sweat. There were about one thousand feet of runway that had been taken up. Most of the units in the area are reporting contact, or having heavy activity. Five marines were firing constantly. The country side was beautiful this morning and evening.

July 9, 1968: Flew 4.3 hours with Captain "J." The squadron off-loaded today to another area. It was not until early in the morning that it was finally decided to go there.

Our X.O. leaves tomorrow to MAG13 and an A-4 squadron. Now to hope for a replacement that is as good.

July 10, 1968: No fly today. Slept until the heat and dust proved unbearable. Chow is outstanding! A big improvement over what we used to eat here.

July 11, 1968: Flew 5.6 hours with "V." Chased the Skipper. Interesting landing!

July 12 1968: SDO, No fly. Squadron beer party.

July 13, 1968: Flew 7.0 hours with "H" on mission. Pretty day.

July 14,1968: Flew 5.6 hours with "V" on mission. Suppose to be hit tonight.

July 15, 1968: No fly.

July 16, 1968: Flew 4.6 hours with Captain "J" on mission. Worked some of the units left around the area. Flew 2.7 hours with Lt. "B" as co-pilot on generals chase, boring!

July 17, 1968: Flew 2.5 hours with Captain "R" as co-pilot. Radio problems. Lost transfer pumps. Changed birds and got an engine chip light. Left the bird and flew home in belly of lead. There is a lot to learn about the UN-34 and flying over here.

July 18, 1968: Flew 5.3 hours. Lt. "S" was co-pilot. On Mission. Bad radios. Got the lead back. Lost engine tact.

July 19, 1968: No fly. Boring!!

July 20, 1968: Flew 3.0 hours with Lt. "B" as co-pilot. Poor radios. We got 1,100 lbs. out of LZ no sweat. Took flight physical this afternoon.

July 21, 1968: Flew 7.2 hours with Lt. "L" as co-pilot. Mission. Chased the Skipper. Lost a Marine today. Crashed and burned. Came close myself today, getting medevacs out of hot area. With a single medevac had to use 3000 rpm go get out. Stated with five. Crashed into trees, lucky to pick a clear spot. "C" thought I had bought it. Went back in and got two passengers and one medevac out, no sweat. The wind probably died down. They were in contact. Had 16 medevacs waiting for us to come get them. No zone, so 46's could not get into the place. It was single wheel for us. Worse zone I have ever seen!

July 22, 1968: Flew 2.8 hours with Lt. "S' as my co-pilot. Back loading the squadron aboard the Princeton. The squadron was aboard in around three hours. Lt "H" is still down because of his wounds. He wants to fly; missing some interesting flying. Good rack tonight.

July 23, 1968: Night medevac. Lt. "S" my co-pilot. Slept late this morning, but managed to get my hair cut and some rolls of film mailed Also started two books. Why can't I do one at a time like most intelligent folks! Making lists, planning our future, etc. The day went quickly.

July 24, 1968: Flew 3.7 hours with Lt. "S" as co-pilot. Supposed to pick up USO show. They were not there! Weather was extremely lousy! Stayed the night at Marble Mt. Saw a Korean band and singers. Girls even! A couple of the guys were kicked out of the "O" Club for excessive celebrating.

July 25, 1968: Flew 2.0 hours again with Lt. "S." He had such a good time I never let him touch the controls! Flew some pax back to the ship. A plane was reported shot down. Another crashed on departure. The weather was again lousy! USO show tonight. Caught up on some sleep.

July 26, 1968: Flew 5.5 hours with Lt. "H" as my co-pilot. Hauled some Army brass around. Our living quarters were flooded this evening. I was sleeping in the room at the time. The sound of the sea water rushing in awoke me. There was about a foot of water on the floor. The squids sealed the compartment off as the compartment above was flooding also. I tried the phone and getting no answer, I decided to bust out as the water had reached my knees and showed no signs of slowing. About this time the ship began to list, and the lights went out. Making my way to the ladder, I lifted the emergency hatch and standing up through the hatchway and reaching one hand up, I found that the water in that compartment was about four feet deep. Closing the emergency hatch, I made my way up to the hanger deck. The squids could not believe I lifted the hatch cover against four feet of salt water. They also said they almost flooded the two compartments completely in their damage control efforts. One time it did pay to get out of the rack. Slept in the junior officer's bunk room.

July 27, 1968: Flew 3.3 hours with Lt. "B." Had radio problems all day! Hauled twelve hundred pounds into a hill. Hauled a medevac out of the lower zone of an LZ. Wearing a borrowed flight suit and boots. The water reached only the lower racks. All the underwear, boots, etc. are soaked.

Still we were very lucky it was not worse. The rooms have not been touched. "P" came back from Sidney today. Aussie girls are as great as everyone says according to him. Have to see for myself. Moved into the junior officer's bunk room.

July 28, 1968: Had night medevac with Lt. "L" Got to square most of my gear away.

July 29, 1968: Had 4.5 hours with Lt. "N." Worked for the 4th Marines. Almost got a chance to call air strikes in. No FM communication between birds. Really a beautiful day.

July 30, 1968: Flew 3.8 hours. Captain "R" was my co-pilot. Hauled the SLF staff around on their daily plane ride. Bought 2/26th the new BLT staff aboard to meet with the ship and SLF. Lousy FM communication again today. Actually not that bad a day. Got the necessary forms for getting some money for our damaged gear.

July 31, 1968: Flew 5.5 hours. Lt. "B" was the co-pilot. Worked for the 9th Marines, the area of the new sweep. The Marines are really digging in. Spent a lot of time shut down waiting on jobs. Stud is very busy as most of the supplies to the hills and units are channeled through here. Finished the month with 130 and some odd hours flying.

August 1, 1968: Flew 6.6 hours with Lt. "W" flying left seat. Had the Da Nang run, mainly just boring. Made two trips. Went under the new mission system today. The Duke got an air medal for his 6.5 hours. 2/26 has requested that we, the Ugly Angels, remain on the float with them.

The N.V.A. have six regiments waiting to cross the DMA and move against (they believe) Dong Ha. General D. reportedly wants 2/26 to come aboard the float early so they will be a floating reserve in case of a big push. We would plug the gap in the DMZ area they would make in their drive south. Would be a hell of a fight!

August 2, 1968: Flew 8.5 hours with Captain "J." Da Nang run and 104 (9ᵗʰ MAR). 5.6 hours for two trips to Da Nang and 2.9 hours at Stud. Had to low level back from Stud due to the rain. Got three new pilots from HMM-163. B.K. crashed today on a downwind landing. Everyone was alright. YL-6 was beat fairly good.

August 3, 1968: Flew 8.2 hours. Lt. "S" was my co-pilot. Worked for the Army and 9ᵗʰ Marines. Got rained out again. The Princeton paper reported that a "white man" was killed while leading a N.V.A. on patrol. He was supposedly wearing utilities, web gear, and carrying an M-14. Also had a red sash around his waist. Wonder who and what he was and what were his reasons and beliefs. I believe Charlie will hit us pretty soon. The battle will be joined as the story book writers say. We will kick his ass again and once again the papers will give Charlie what he could not gain on the battlefield. We are running huge convoys every direction. Supplies are flooding in. Good to see some form of support from the "good old U.S.A.!"

August 4, 1968: No fly. A day off; hell of a waste of a good day. Got the order out to the Hong Kong branch of Winchester. Also started completing the order to Remington. Had a lift of 2/26's people back to Quang Tri this evening. Seems someone put some of 2/26 on the float without getting approval. Started Stone's "Those Who Love" and feel there will be no problem keeping interested.

August 5, 1968: Flew 5.2 hours with Commander "Y" as co-pilot. Had the C&C birds from the 12ᵗʰ Marines. Weather was really lousy. Lost all radio communication and had to return to the ship. Relaunched in the afternoon for one hour. Two ships hit each other tonight. One man is believed missing overboard.

August 6, 1968: Flew 5/7 hours with Captain "E" as co-pilot. In country medevac and SLF C&C birds. Bought 2/26 people aboard today. There is an operation in the works as soon as 2/26 can draw up the plans and write the necessary orders. The weather has begun to turn lousy, especially late in the afternoon in the mountains.

August 7, 1968: Flew 1.8 hours with Captain "R" as co-pilot. Night medevac birds. We were launched to Da Nang late in the afternoon to take the D.M. and pick up the SIX in charge of the SLF. The SIX was not supposed to arrive until early on the eighth. A lot of brass around. It took four Huey's to carry them all. Spent the night at Marble Mt.

August 8, 1968: Flew 1.4 hours with Captain "R" as co-pilot. Did a pickup at LZ 11 at 0630 and flew back to the ship. Sent in our order to Remington Arms. Flew 1.0 hour with Lt. "V" as co-pilot. Went into Dong Ha with mail and V.R. the landing zone for the coming strike. Flew 1.0

Hour with Lt. "N" as co-pilot. Went over to the Dubuque for great chow. Then briefed their 4.2 mortar platoon on the UH-34. Had a complete radio failure in YL-16. Not a bad day for an off day.

August 9, 1969: His views on how to save South Vietnam!

Another off day. Not too bad, however, because of the preparations for this strike exercise. Practice for the real thing. The air cavalry has gone back into action. Finally their mobility is being used. The mailed fist that strikes at enemy concentrations, destroying troops and supplies and then is gone. We need more of these operations to give Charlie no secure base areas and turn him into a hunted animal. We have to do a lot more work, however! This is but one step on a long road leading to a brighter tomorrow for Vietnam and her people. Next, we must isolate the N.F.L. from the people politically. Then the government must come forward and take the reins of control in the rural areas. Schools, medical aid, help for the farmers, in short; the RVE must get its roots deep into the population of Vietnam. It must become "of the people," "for the people," "by the people." Once this begins, we jump on the V.C. hard. Those that do not turn themselves in are hunted down and destroyed. This is how we can win in Vietnam. Start at the bottom and build slowly, but surely, up until a stable government that represents the people results. No matter what form the government takes!

August 10, 1968: Flew 5.9 hours today. Lt. "N" was copilot. We put the BLT ashore. Everything went quite smoothly. We had twenty-one birds up for the strike. For the morning's first launch the birds of two separate divisions were mixed. The result was a hectic few minutes until everyone was joined up properly. Then they tried exercising control over four divisions lifting into a zone only ten minutes away. Results were badly overloaded radio nets; a lot of useless information being sent. They also did not load the first wave to its full capacity. The combat cargo crews did not know the proper method of rigging external loads. (One mule I was lifting turned over splashing gasoline all over the deck. I had to set the mule back down, doing it no good.) and the (-) did not know the proper signals. Our new (-) made a good many mistakes today. We went on the strike with no radios (breaking briefing rule). No one had been assigned to take division leader, and when it was passed, it was given to a new HAC. We went too slow into the zone, landing in the wrong area, and too much speed straight and level. Some of us would have been killed had the zone been hot.

The basic plan was as follows: Amphibious landing of troops and armor. This wave moves inland, secures an LZ, and we bring in the mortar teams and other heavy equipment. I had squadron duty tonight.

August 11, 1968: SDO today. Slept all day making up for last night. BLT back loaded today. Got my order blanks for our Fisher Amplifier.

August 12, 1968: Flew 4.6 hours with Lt. "V" as co-pilot. Worked for the 4th MAR. The weather was so lousy we had to 'incomplete' the mission. We were nearly blind because the wipers did not work. Had to low level back to Camp Carroll, along Route 9 from Stud. Ceiling was around fifty feet with rain. Took some medevacs out to the Repose on our way back to the tub. Secured for the day once we made it back here. Today was the squadron's seventh day without mail.

(What it takes to be a HAC: Awareness of surroundings, knowing varied combat approaches, use of radio communication, self-confidence, but not over confidence, and never growing lax.) I must always work on my flying and never grow lax!

August 13, 1968: Had night medevac with Lt. "N" as co-pilot. Finished book "Those Who Love," today. Damn good book! Must buy the hard cover version. Started "The Best Times" by Dos Passos. It is strengthening my desire to see and to try to understand life and things about me.

August 14, 1968: Flew 7.3 hours with Lt. "D" as co-pilot. Had working birds for the 3rd and 1st Marines. Took a N.V.A. who surrendered up above A-4 where he pointed out his regiments location. The N.V.A. seemed very young and frightened. He had long, uncombed black hair and was very small even for a Vietnamese. Dressed in clean civilian clothes and sporting a size small flack-jacket, he seemed attached to his guard in an animal like fashion, even when everyone was very kind. We flew north, close to North Vietnam. "B" got shot up between A-3 and A-4 taking one hit. We took three air bursts at C-4, no hits.

August 15, 1968: Flew 2.4 hours with Lt. "R" as co-pilot. Had the practice strike against area just south of location. Put a rifle platoon in on the LZ in the morning and brought them back in the afternoon. The troops were on board the Dubuque which sat about a mile off shore. Had to stand by all day with a reserve company in case of trouble. They tested us and we were ready to go in six and one-half minutes. Got some good pictures. The BLT and SLF were very pleased with the Squadron's work.

August 16, 1968: Flew 6.0 hours with Lt. "V." Had the Danang mail run. No letters today. Flew SAR and TAO for afternoon portion of the landing exercise. Flew close formation while low leveling. We struck at the regiment near the DMZ that the N.V.A. prisoner pointed out. I guess we really got a hot one. F-4's worked the area over and were still drawing heavy fire after an hour. A CH-46 with a recon team was shot up when it tried to land. One crew saw around 10 zips in the general area. "B" and "V" went in and extracted a recon team and the crew of a crashed UH-1E.

August 17, 1968: Flew 1/5 hours with Lt. "H" in the left seat. Same old exercise. The weather was real poor this afternoon—five hundred feet in rain. Two F-4 jocks ejected up near Tiger Island because the bad weather had closed down all airfields capable of landing them. Jolly Greens picked them up shortly after splash down. We turned two birds just in case. Received word tonight that tomorrow we put the BLT ashore near the DMZ.

General opinion is that we will lose some people. The gooks have plenty of fifties, mortars, and artillery up there. Should be interesting. I believe in a hot zone like that we will be lucky to get everyone back. We will do our jobs just like we always do. A lot of gooks will wish they never heard of the U.S.M.C.

August 18, 1968: Flew 4.2 hours with Lt. "V" in the left seat. Put the BLT ashore today in the 1ˢᵗ Marines' positions. The 1ˢᵗ Marines (a battalion) will conduct a raid. By the time we were supposed to take off, we still did not know where the initial company would be dropped. I flew slot man on the lead division. Flying a diamond can be pure hell. During normal cruise one cannot fly too fast and must wait for the division to form up. Approaches must not begin too far from the zone and not too slow. Radio procedures and headwork must be above par. These are the requirements when going into a hot zone. To do everything right and still buy it, is one of the breaks; but to die uselessly, God help us. I PRAY I CAN ALWAYS DO IT RIGHT.

August 19, 1968: Day off! Started reading "Hell in a Very Small Place," by Fall. Very interesting. Nearly everything I read and see makes me believe that my view on Viet Nam is basically sound. Received the first mail for a long while. Really caught up on my sleep. "F.E." returned today. Wife and little girl are doing well.

August 20, 1968: Flew 5.6 hours today with Lt." S" riding left seat. Working birds for the BLT. Flew a couple of VR's up to about the DMZ at low level. Spotted N.V.A. and could not get them to shoot so we could gun them. Rain showers this afternoon. Our troops are moving nearly everywhere. Glad to see it. We are looking for contact now, pushing Charlie into a corner where he has to fight. Then we beat their brains in!

August 21, 1968: Flew 3.7 hours with Lt. "C" in the left seat. Partial backload of BLT 2/26. Lifted "G" Company out, 81mm mortar PLT, 106 recoilless rifle PLT; and A and B command groups. "F" Company is to be left in field overnight. Once again confusion reigned as the 1ˢᵗ Marines did not arrive on time to relieve the units of 2/26. The SLF and BLT staffs had it well in hand but no one could explain things to the Navy.

August 22, 1968: Flew 3.8 hours with Lt. "W" as Co-pilot. Backloaded "F" Company today. Chased the lead again today.

August 23, 1968: Flew 5.4 hours with Captain "H." Had 4th Marines working birds. Was really impressed with the changes that have taken place since I was last there. The scrub land to the east of C.C. shows the tracks of countless armored vehicles. C.C. has been beefed up with new wire, trenches, and tanks dug in on the line. The route is beginning to look like a highway back in the States. Stud is really digging in with a good underground bunker complex and are clearing wide fields of fire. Flew supplies into "B" Company today. They were just southeast. In contact with the dead, in the zone. The faces of the dead do not have the harried, tired and lost look of the living. Maybe they have found something better. Captain "D" and "P" crashed today.

They hit a fallen tree. Burst the center fuel cell, and cracked the skin and a couple of ribs. Flew it back to the ship.

August 24, 1968: Flew 5.4 hours with Lt. "N" flying left seat. Da Nang mail run. The fight for Da Nang has started. The Hog got me into blade stall today. Made it out alive, just barely! Flew for the super grunts. Worked with the Awards Board.

August 25, 1968: No fly. Got in 2.6 hours on a lift into Streeter of "G" Company. Lt. "L" was co-pilot. Had three out of four birds shot up north of C-2. Lt. "P" crashed in the zone, but Lt. "N" got everyone out all right.

August 26, 1968: Flew 7.4 hours with Lt. "V" in the left seat. Working birds for 4th and 9th Marines. Took two mortar rounds while sitting on top of 950; no hits. Fixed wing immediately jumped on the site. During my next trip into 950, an F-4 made two passes under me keeping their heads down. UH-46's would not go in. We told them to get back and let some Marines do the job. Good day!

August 27, 1968: Flew 4.9 hours. Commander "Y" was my Co-pilot. Flew 2.0 hours on a shuttle between Streeter and the tub. Worked for DASC during the afternoon lifting troops north. General impression we are setting in better. The DMZ and area south of it is being swept more regularly. We are also in the mountains.

August 28, 1968: Day off! Entire 2/26 put ashore at D-5. Only two crews off. Charlie is supposed to be concentrated north. Sorry to miss the strike.

August 29, 1968: Flew 5.3 hours with Lt. "V" in the left seat. Finished the ferrying or 2/26 ashore to D-5.

August 30, 1968: Flew t.1 hours with Lt. "L" in left seat. Medevac and C&C for SLF.

August 31, 1968: Flew 4.7 hours with Lt. "C" in the left seat Medevac and ARG shuttle run.

Picked up Captain.

September 1, 1968: Night Medevac with Lt. "S" in left seat. No launch.

September 2, 1968: Flew 1.8 hours with Lt. "N" as Co-pilot. Off loaded the Ugly Angels at Marble Mt. Took us about four hours. My bird went down with control problems. Had a good hooch, hot as hell, no fans or A/C.

September 3, 1968: Condition IV for night Medevac in case first team gets shot up (three times in last week) or more than six hours. Cleaned up the hooch. Went to S-2 brief tonight. Suppose to be hottest area in Viet Nam right now. Can hear incoming aways to our south. Enemy battle plans call for probing attacks and harassment fire until an assault during TET. Marines are sweeping all around the area. Real mobile! Our XO seems to be taking over more and more. Two birds were shot up on night Medevac.

September 4, 1968: Flew 1.2 hours with Lt. "F." I flew left seat for an area checkout. Bird was damaged on take-off. Last time I sign for a bird and fly left seat! Lousy weather, less than five hundred feet. Captain "C" got shot up two times on day Medevac. We were mortared (one round) at 0530. We are on condition III again.

September 5, 1968: Flew 4.0 hours with Captain "B" in the left seat. Typhoon hit today. Flight operations were secured except for Medevac. Around a third of our roof was town off. Launched out at 0130 and did not get back until 0530. Took fire north of Song An Hoa. Got out three emergency Medevacs. Weather was not too bad. Captain "O" was shot up three times.

September 6, 1968: Condition IV. Slept the day through.

September 7 1968: SDO

September 8, 1968: SDO. Learned that I took two hits. One in the spar and the other in a blade pocket; during night Medevac the 5th of September. Missed the USO show at the club tonight. Had some round eyes in it.

September 9, 1968: Flew 1.4 hours with Lt. "B" in the left seat. Chased a Huey to Phu Bai and back with a load of V.I.P.'s for LZ 300. Had the first of daily 0800 APM's. Received an outstanding letter from Brent today. The only thing I regret is being away from her. My job is very necessary and is making me a better man; but, I miss her. I am taking over Career Advisory tomorrow. I am at fault for being behind the eight ball as far as collateral duties are concerned.

The X.O. jumped in my face about this; much as I hate to say it he is right, and I am wrong. Just finished reading "Marine" tonight. We still have not learned in many cases. General Puller (Author) bitches about the same things we are bitching about today. Saw in my log book that I was made a section leader the 31st of August. The squadron is also making eight new HAC's. "P" is one of them. Got my Nomex flight suits. What I need now is a clear visor, and I should be all set for flight equipment. (I will hold off on leather flight jacket and second set of flight boots) Got my warrant signed by S-1 and now only need to get the appropriate copies to MAG-16 disbursing. I find it hard to see the logic in the fighting down here.

September 10, 1968: Flew .8 of an hour with Major "S" in left seat. Generals chase and a .3 single pilot returning a down aircraft from LZ400 to Marble Mt. Captain "B" and Lt. "F" were both shot at today.

September 11, 1968: Flew 2.3 hours left seat with Captain "D." Pickup hop VIP run down to LZ 465 and back. Out of the four pilots, had one division leader and three section leaders doing what really amounted to nothing. Small arms fire to the southwest of LZ 465. Hill 65 does not look like too hard a nut to crack. It has an Army 175 section, Marine 155's and 105's. OV-10 and F-4's working out on an area two miles south.

September 12, 1968: Flew 2.7 hours with Lt. "B" in the left seat. Had morning Medevac. Picked up a total of four emergencies, four priorities, and three routes. First pickup was in the area I watched being hit the day before. Lost A.S.E, I.C.S. communications, and miscellaneous other things (Ma-1 compass) on the way to the zone. Grunts threw on four medevacs and too much equipment. Bit touchy here and there getting out. Had to crash through a couple of hedges to get out. Huey "gun" got all excited with me working around looking for a way out. Lucky Charlie was not close by! Picked up a NVA in bad shape later in the day. Charlie hit Marble Mt. last night. We went on condition 11A (enemy contact probable). The Huey's and Spookie worked out.

September 13, 1968: Day off. Represented squadron at Mag-16 Change Of Command. Joined Uni Club Inc. today. I should be due for night Medevac pretty soon.

September 14, 1968: Flew 1.9 hours as Co-pilot with Captain "B" on General's chase. Got 0.6 hours on a night test hop with Lt. "V" left seat. Got 1 Major three N.F.G's today. Two of the new people moved in. Got put on night Medevac. Have to pull my share.

September 15, 1968: Hop cancelled. Reading "The Soldier and the Sage." Interesting!

September 16, 1968: Flew 6.3 hours with Lt. "D" and Lt. "B" as co-pilots. Worked for the Korean Marines. Very interesting people. Quite a few were big men, even in our standards. Their positions are extremely well fortified. Must get to know them better. See some new area maybe. Not much remains to be studied.

September 17, 1968: Day off. Boring day. Four of our pilots will go for FAC next month.

September 18, 1968: No fly. Got 1.0 in night bounce pattern. Lead bird on a night Medevac crashed in a zone and burned. Gooks opened up with .50 caliber fire and R.P.G.'s or recoilless rifle fire. Chase was unable to go into the zone. Spooky and some gunships worked the area and a UH-46 got everyone out a half hour later.

"B" and I took overnight Medevac. Lt. "V" flew left seat. Lt. "S" badly burned his hands, wearing no gloves, left side of his face burned, and assorted cuts. Gunner took a round in the hip. Everyone else got out with burns and cuts. We got 1.8 hours.

September 19, 1968: Had night Medevac. Capt. "R" was Co-pilot and he did an excellent job. Got 4.3 hours and hauled 13 Medevacs. One grenade wounded died in the aircraft. I think I did the best possible; but what would his parents or wife think? Took a round in the oil cooler armor plate on the first pickup. A bit higher and either "B" or I would have been hit. Twice the grunts had the Medevacs between me and the light marking the zone. Had to use lights, something I dislike doing. Lt. "S" and his crew were sent by Medevac to Japan.

September 20, 1968: Condition IV. Got 1.2 hours with Captain "R" as Co-pilot. Night Medevac got only an hour.

September 21, 1968: Flew 1.9 hours with Lt. "H" flying left seat. General's chase to Phu Bai and back. Charlie hit us tonight. Our squadron has two birds flying, one with battle damage. Group had fifty birds hit. Big fire fight southwest perimeter.

September 22, 1968: Day off! Rainy day. Took some pictures of the damage. Around five rounds hit our line.

September 23, 1968: Flew 5.6 hours afternoon Medevac. Major "P" our new X.O. flew left seat. We were pretty busy, only shut down once. I broke a tail wheel locking pin, my second. The Major shook me a couple of times. I guess Charlie has not made a believer out of him yet. He likes to fly low and slow out over Indian country. I do not! "P" has his first night Medevac as HAC tonight.

September 24, 1968: Flew .7 with Lt. "H" in the left seat. Had condition II & IV. Another all night haul in the ready room. The heavies are taking day Medevac per usual. The C.O. has had it six mornings in a row. Naturally, he does not fly night Medevac. This chicken shit business is pissing me off. I have had day Medevac only twice (Had to complain to get that!) and have had night Medevac five times. If I can fly night Medevac that many times, I should get day Medevac at least as many times. Since "S" crashed, the heavies have flown night Medevac only once.

September 25, 1968: Today off. Have four FAC's to come from us. MAG-16 got six and sent four to HM-362.

September 26, 1968: Flew 2.3 hours with Lt. "B" in the left seat. Chased the General around the area. Ate chow at Hill 55, excellent. For most of the time we were not needed as we only left the Danang complex once.

September 27, 1968: Day off.

September 28, 1968: Day off. Flew to Chu Lai for SAR duty in a UN-46. Nervous as hell! Do not live very good down here.

September 29, 1968: Flew 1.0 hour with Lt. "B" in left seat. Shot every type of approach could think of. Boring! Like to watch A-4's. Really would like to fly them.

September 30, 1968: Flew 0.5 hours with Lt. "H" left seat. Tried to shoot some GCA's, but the weather was closing in and the jets needed it more than I.

October 1, 1968: Flew 1.0 hour with Lt. "B" left seat. Back to Marble Mt. Lt. Col. "S" lost his turns and crashed today on a hoist Medevac pickup. Learned that four men are going to JAC school. Flew 4.5 hours with Lt. "V" left seat on night medevac. Had two unsecure zones. Not that bad! First unsecure zone. The grunts turned off the light in the zone once I was below tree level. That was worse than the fire I drew going in and coming out. Man it is dark down there! Also drew fire in route to the zone. Three fire incidents on one Medevac.

October 2, 1968: Had condition IV. Did not launch.

October 3, 1968: Flew 2.3 hours with Major "A" left seat. Mission two. The Major's first in-country hop in a UH34.

October 4, 1968: No fly! October 5, 1968: No fly!

October 6, 1968; Took the instrument test today with "P." Took six and one-half hours. We sent five men to HML-167 or VMO-1. I wanted to, but they would not let me.

October 7, 1968: Flew 3.0 hours of morning Medevac with Captain "E." Tried a hoist pickup of a wounded recon almost where Lt. Col. Crashed. The recon heard voices and movement ten meters out of the zone. Tried three times and could not hover; had to wave-off over expected VC/NVA base camp. Drew fire the second wave off. Hated to leave the kid, but he was not an emergency, and I could not hack it. I chopped the tops of a few trees trying, but the H-34 was not meant to do hovering at a thousand feet out of ground effect and out of wind. A Navy Captain was my Doc today.

October 8, 1968: Flew 9.6 hours with Lt. "P" in the left seat. Had C&C for the 7th Marines at Hill 55. Flew in Thuong Duc a couple of times. Constant air strikes and artillery missions. Charlie is supposed to be around the area in force (about three regiments). We are sweeping with two Marine battalions and one ARVN battalion. Charlie is dug in, but good. UH-46 was shot out of the drop zone the first day. Lt. "N" had his jeep blown up by an explosive packet thrown into or planted on it. The driver was hurt.

October 9, 1968: SDO today. Two UH-46's crashed. Everyone alright. Flew 0.3 hours to bring back YL-19 from General's pad. It had boast pump problems.

October 10, 1968: Slept most of the day. Attended ISO meeting at Group. HMM was used as a good example, so I guess we are not too bad off.

October 11, 1968: CAPTAIN STEVEN W. MARTIN, USMCR, died in a mid-air collision with another helicopter. Fourteen young men did not survive the crash.

NAMES AND DETAILS of the day may be found at USMC/ Combat Helicopter Association POP-A-SMOKE Incident Date 681011 HMM-362 UH-34D 148802 and HMM-265 CH-46A 151917 Mid-air Collision. Or, http://www.popasmoke.com/kia/incidents. php?incidentid=187.

The Shattering Of A Family

Chapter 9

The Shattering Of A Family

As previously mentioned, December 13, 1967 was Christmas Day for the Martin family. It was a successful attempt at normalcy as Steve had gone into town after the festivities; and for a moment, he had wondered why so many stores were open and so many people were out and about!

Steve and Brent had rented a house in a neighboring town, and much to the angst of the landlord, they moved out after only three months. Maybe he didn't understand that when one applies and accepts Uncle Sam's invitation, you can't say "no thanks." Much to Brent's relief, Steve had made arrangements for her to live with his parents while he was away.

Brent found a receptionist job at a medical clinic, and at home, especially enjoyed the company of Steve's mother. She enjoyed shopping excursions, family events, learning to paint with oils, and the day to day activities, etc. Dad Martin did write in one letter to Steve for him to hurry home. "These women were driving him nuts!"

Sunday, October 13, 1968 was a beautiful New England autumn day. Mother Martin had prepared a very nice brunch, and the family had eaten in the dining room together, rather than separately as their work schedules usually dictated.

After the meal, Brent was walking down the hallway when she saw there were two men coming in the door who wanted to speak to her.

Brent saw the military uniform. The other man introduced himself as a Chaplain, and they asked her to sit down. She heard her voice saying: NO, NO, NO! Probably it was the Chaplain's voice she heard say: "She knows. Say the words." A thought was in Brent's head that maybe he was only wounded, but then they would not be there if that was the reason. She heard the words---that shattered her life and those of the Martin family. "Captain Steven W. Martin died..." His image flashed before her eyes and she continued to hear her own voice saying: "NO, NO, NO!

Through her tears she looked up and saw her brother, Wayne, enter the room. At no time during her living at the Martin's had he visited her before. There had been no time for anyone to have notified him of Steve's death. He had just decided to visit that Sunday.

He tried to console her and suggested he take her to their parents to let them know. The tears would not stop, and on the way to her parent's house she admonished herself that she had to get control of her emotions, as she didn't want to upset her mother more than necessary. She had seen her mother collapse, in church, from a CVA when she was about six years old. Her grief had to be contained for her mother's sake.

Her parents were consoling, and Brent was taken back to the Martin's by her brother; to start living with the knowledge that her life would never be the same again.

The days leading up to the funeral were indescribable. Brent will never be able to express enough appreciation for the arrival of Captain Ski, the Marine Corps officer sent to help the family through the day. His strong presence will never be forgotten. His white gloved hand steadied her and gave her the courage to calmly honor Steve that day.

N

Brent recalled one evening as Steve was completing his flight training, and they were living in Jacksonville, North Carolina. He had received his orders to go to Vietnam. She knew this is what he had been training for the last two years, but her fears had surfaced. In his words to console her he said: "You will be okay." He never said: "I will be okay."

N

The winter of 1969 was one that had produced a lot of snow and very high snow banks along the road by the little brown house (camp, per Steve) that Brent now owned alone. She was planning to move out of her in-laws home and into it when the ice and snow melted away in the spring. It was a month or so after the new year that those plans were suddenly altered by her father-in-law.

Dad Martin and Mother Martin were talking together when Brent approached them. The first words she recalls hearing were about moving out. Dad Martin then turned to Brent and said: "And, you are on your own!" These words stung as Brent was very much aware of the fact that she was now on her own.

THE LITTLE BROWN HOUSE

OCTOBER 1970 THE LITTLE BROWN HOUSE

MARCH 1969 THE PATH TO THE FRONT DOOR AND THE 1969 CAMERO

Brent made plans to move into the little brown house as soon as possible. Her brother came up and shoveled the huge snow bank, in front of the walkway leading up to the entrance of the house. It had been pushed up there by the snow plows. Electricity and water were turned on, and furnishings were acquired from Brent's parents. The heating system was totally inadequate; but Dad Martin, being in the heating business, did replace the system for her.

Dad Martin also wanted Brent to trade her car for a better model. He set out to school her in the art of purchasing a car. He went with her to a dealership, and she observed as he listened to the salesman's pitch. Thinking that he was satisfied with the deal, Brent was surprised when he thanked the salesman, and as they walked out the door he turned to her and said: "There, that is how it is done."

A few days later he suggested she go to another dealership. Brent asked him if he was going with her, and he answered in the negative. Brent went to the dealership alone. Good deal or not, she left with a new 1969 Chevrolet Camaro. Brent had been "schooled" on being independent.

It was quite some time later when Mother Martin was able to confide to Brent what was going on with Dad that horrible winter of 1969. Even though he appeared on the outside to be coping, everything reminded him of his son. He wanted to rid himself of everything and everyone, including her. Thanks to her strength and love, she was able to save her marriage and bring the family back together.

Brent lived in the little brown house from the winter of 1969 to the spring of 1971 when she relocated to St. Petersburg, Florida. She only visited Pensacola, Florida one time; where she and Steve had lived the longest of their married life.

In Memory of Steven Wayne Martin,
Captain, U.S.M.C. 1943-1968

This memorial is the work of Eileen Martin, Captain Martin's mother. A copy was added to each book, donated to the public library, in his name.

Chapter 10

The Tribute Letters

Letters in tribute to Captain Steven W. Martin from his and Brent's friends: Each one expressed a special principle of Steve's or how we were all enriched with having had him in our lives.

I always smile when I read my friend Betty's words: "Despite the sadness you now face, I know that you would rather have experienced those few years with Steve, than never to have known him at all." How very true.

And, a letter from an unknown person to Brent, expressing a mother's pride in her young son and hoping to have the strength to say the right thing, should he ever be asked to serve his country.

What a beautiful letter from Peter Miner. A man strong enough to allow himself to weep over the loss of his friend.

Another friend, Peter Pohl, expressing the value of Steve's friendship.

Every thought, letter, card and note of condolence was received with gratitude to the sender; even after all these years. Thanks to all of you for your comforting words.

Most sincerely, Brent.

> 'Lord, guard and guide the men who fly
> through the great spaces of the sky.
> Be with them traversing the air,
> In darkening storm or sunshine fair.'

14 October 1968: Dear Brent, Often as a cadet I took a great deal of comfort in this hymn, and even now in the moment of the greatest sorrow and loss that I have ever experienced, I find the words reassuring, for I am confident that He was with him in the 'darkening storm' which took Steve from us on this earth.

There are many words that come to mind at the moment, but most are trite and hollow, and the rest I think you know I am thinking. I feel a special closeness to you tonight, Brent, for we are two of the few who knew him best and loved him most—have seen him light up when flying was the topic of conversation. I always regarded your husband as closer than a brother to me, ever since we first met, but the love of flying which came later cemented an already inseparable bond between us. (I'll never forget the way you all just sat back resigned whenever we got going on stories.)

And before I ever knew you—from the time I knew of you, I have had a special respect for the person that I knew you must be, to be loved by the man who I held dearest in this world. After a couple of years of getting to know more of you, I know that my faith in Steve was more than warranted and accurate, for you are a very strong girl and one who could live with the decision he made.

Now you are being called on to summon up every last ounce of that strength, to face this loss as he would have had it. His was a brave and dangerous job, and he was a strong person, yet he too broke down at some of the losses.

This evening, for the first time in many, many years, I could no longer laugh-yah, I couldn't even smile, and I am not the least ashamed—I cried. Even now I can barely see to write through the tears. Outwardly they shall pass, but the hurt lives on, and this is the truest test of strength which I know is yours, and which I know Steve counted on in his friends and family. As the wound begins to throb a bit less, I pray that we may gather ourselves and press on in our lives, still of use to our fellow men. Let us try even harder to make the world a better place, each of us in his own small way. Steve was fighting for a cause he believed in to the best of my knowledge, and one which isn't getting all the support from home that it might have.

Just as soon as I can get out of this assignment, I intend to get on over and try to do my share to support the cause he died for.

There are so many more words that I want to say, but even now it's a bit jumbled. Forgive the disorder, and keep your chin up. I'll write later when I'm a bit more organized. Be sure and let me know as soon as you can, any details, and I'll try to be up if it can be done.

Please give my best to all the family. My prayers are with them too, but this I had to write to you. Yours, Pete. (Miner)

(Brent remembers Pete standing at Steven's graveside, in uniform, at attention and saluting as she was driven away from the ceremony at the cemetery.)

October 18, 1968: Dear Brent, You have been in my thoughts constantly ever since Richard brought me the terrible news which shocked the entire community. Words seem so helpless at a time like this, yet I had to write and try to express my feelings.

Friendship is so often taken for granted until you have lost a friend and you suddenly realize the full impact of this loss. Few events in my life have had such a profound effect on me as Steve's tragic death has. Both Richard and I commented last night that Steve was like a brother to us both. I first met Steve at U.N.H. Our first encounter resulted in a friendship, the loss of which will have a profound effect on me for a long time to come. His warmth and friendly personality were an inspiration to us all. I shall cherish the fond memories of our dormitory life. The all night discussions on numerous topics had a particular significance. We seemed to have very similar views, a fact which strengthened our friendship. I recall with fond memories the night you and Sue came to U.N.H. and we went out for dinner and then proceeded to the pool room at U.N.H., where I naturally came in last. Our nightly marathons and weight lifting episodes provided a welcome break from the tedious academic life.

Steve's deep devotion and pride towards his country left the greatest impression on me. Casting personal interests aside; he went to serve his country as a member of an elite outfit. Steve never settled for second best. I think this was one of his basic philosophies. It at least applied in his choice of a military branch and more importantly in his choice for a wife.

Recently I heard that today's college generation is more concerned with finding a challenge in life rather than measuring success in terms of monetary earning. I think this is true in many cases. I know it is for me and my impression was that Steve felt much the same. Most of us desire to contribute something to society during our lifetime.

During the last nine months Steve accomplished more than millions do during their entire life. I can't think of a greater reward than having aided in saving hundreds of lives. Each survivor is a living memorial to the ideals which Steve lived for and for which he made the greatest sacrifice possible.

I hope that somehow you can find the strength and courage to cope with your loss. Time is essential for this to occur. The fond memories which you must have will help and the fact that Steve was participating in something he truly believed in also helps in a small way. I shall miss him very much.

If there is anything I can do, don't hesitate to ask.

A friend, Peter (Pohl)

Fall 1968: Dear Brenda, I wish I could offer you some great comfort at this time of sorrow, but my words are inadequate. I can only express my deepest sympathy to you and those who loved Steve. I did not know Steve well, but that he was a wonderful person is reflected by the path of life he followed.

Despite the sadness you now face, I know that you would rather have experienced those few years with Steve, then never to have known him at all. If there is anything I can do to be of help to you, please ask. Very Sincerely, Betty Spongberg (Keister)

FROM THE SENATE JOURNAL, N.H.

WEDNESDAY, FEBRUARY 19, 1969

Sen. Spanos moved the Senate go into the late session and when it adjourns today, it adjourn in honor of those intrepid U.S. Marines who stormed the shores of Iwo Jima 24 years ago, and in honor of Captain Steven Martin of Moultonborough who flew 948 missions over Viet Nam before being killed in action.

Tuesday, 22 October, 1968: Dear Brent, Just a note to extend my heartfelt and sincerest sympathy to you and to say you are in my thoughts and prayers.

I know of your great pride in your husband; of a young man who loved his family and his Country enough to offer himself to a cause he believed to be just and right, and you must know that his life was not given in vein.

Though our son is only three- and one-half, I try to visualize how the world will be when he reaches service age. If, when he is of military age, his services will be needed to help keep us in the United States secure and free; and yes, even to fight for those persons who lack pride in self and country. I will be a very, very proud person. To be sure, I will have a mother's fears and questions; but with God's help, I will have the strength to do and say the right thing.

Brent, I am doing a very poor job of trying to express what is in my heart for you, but please know you are not now, nor ever will be, alone.

You have memories which are very precious, and that no one can ever take away. You also have gained a richness and fulfillment from these past three years, that in the future will have great meaning: May God bless you at this time, and may He be always at your side.

With great fondness, "C" (Unknown to Brent. Signed only first name.)

THE NEWS, MEREDITH, N.H. NOVEMBER 13, 1969

MOULTONBORO—Last Friday evening, Nov. 7th, Mrs. Steven Martin and Mrs. Harold Martin were in Portsmouth at the Marine Corps Barracks to accept the Bronze Star Medal with Combat "V" and the air Medal with the number 40, awarded posthumously to Captain Steven Wayne Martin, their husband and son. The Air Medal with the numeral 40 signified that he had earned forty medals, each medal requiring twenty missions, and that he had flown eight hundred missions.

The Presidential citation reads as follows:

The President of the United States takes pride in presenting the Bronze Star Medal posthumously to Captain Steven Wayne Martin, United States Marine Corps Reserve for services set forth in the following citation:

"For meritorious service in connection with operations against the enemy in the Republic of Vietnam while serving with Marine Medium Helicopter Squadron 362, Marine Aircraft Group Sixteen, First Marine Aircraft Wing from 28 December 1967, to 11 October 1968. Throughout this period, Captain Martin performed his demanding duties in an exemplary manner. Although assigned primary duty as a Pilot, he served additionally as a Post Maintenance Inspector and demonstrated superb leadership and technical knowledge while consistently providing his command with outstanding support. Working tirelessly and with meticulous attention to detail, he skillfully trained and supervised his men to increase their proficiency, thereby greatly enhancing the efficiency and effectiveness of his section.

Displaying exceptional initiative and resolute determination, he contributed significantly to his squadron's performance by ensuring that friendly units in Hue City and near the Khe Sanh Combat Base received timely resupply missions. Constantly striving for perfection, he participated in an off-duty technical educational program that involved a comprehensive study of publications and flight manuals concerning the maintenance and operation of helicopters. His determined efforts and tireless initiative were an inspiration to all who served with him and contributed immeasurably to the accomplishment of his unit's mission. Captain Martin's professionalism, super resourcefulness and steadfast devotion to duty throughout were in keeping with the highest traditions of the Marine Corps and of the United States Naval Services."

The Marine Corps is celebrating its anniversary at this time of year. Mrs. Steven Martin attended the Anniversary Ball and was in Dover for the Veteran's Day observance held in that city.

Captain Martin was killed in Vietnam on October 11, 1968 when his helicopter was in a collision with another helicopter.

PRESENTATION OF MEDALS FOR CAPTAIN STEVEN W. MARTIN TO HIS WIFE

The ARSE Intact Awards

Steve would occasionally make a comment about "Keeping his ARSE intact so far," during his Marine training.

Upon remembering this, Brent started buying gifts for him each month he was in Vietnam. One month it might be a book about his interests in wildlife or forestry, other months about history or aviation. Objects such as a hunting knife, a compass, a duck whistle, or fishing gear would be included. These were to be his "ARSE-INTACT AWARDS" to be presented to him upon his return home.

Brent doesn't remember what became of these items. Maybe the books were given to the town library in his memory. Other things may have been left in his room when Brent moved out of his parent's house; and only removed when after Dad Martin's death, when his mother sold the house.

IN MEMORY OF A SON,
BROTHER, HUSBAND,
AND RESIDENT OF
MOULTONBORO, N.H.

STEVEN WAYNE MARTIN
CAPTAIN, U.S.M.C.
11/02/1943 to 10/11/1968

Town Memorial

WIDOWHOOD AND MOUNTAIN CLIMBING

Chapter 11

Widowhood And Mountain Climbing

Widow: An Indo-European root meaning
'be empty,' or Latin 'bereft.'

In the months and a few years after Steve's death, Brent had friends who talked her into going skiing or mountain climbing.

On one sunny, summer day the red headed boy, who was a former classmate, talked her into going mountain climbing.

After a fairly easy climb, they stopped and sat on a huge bolder to enjoy the view and to engage in conversation. In the conversation he referred to her as an "emotional cripple!" Brent resented this, as after the initial weeks after the funeral and upon returning to work, she had wanted to appear to be strong and to "carry on" as Steve would have wanted. In thinking back, the red headed boy saw through the façade, and was describing his own emotional state, as well as hers. He had been there and done that, as he was a veteran.

Brent was to go on a couple of other mountain "adventures," and one of them entailed riding up the ski lift and, of course, skiing back down the mountain. Well, on the particular day the slopes were actually rather icy. Brent should have stayed on the beginner's slope. The one thought was that if she crashed, her friend Sonny Stern, a lab technician at work, would be able to maybe put the pieces back together for her family.

In thinking back, maneuvering that ski slope was as slippery as maneuvering in the role of being a widow, at the age of twenty-three. The mountain was too steep, the icy snow was too slippery. There were moguls and trees looming up to be maneuvered around. Just like her new life, do this, don't do that...!

The last mountain climbing adventure for Brent was with Steve's friend, Richard Wakefield, their best man on their wedding day. The climb was more steep and difficult for Brent as they progressed upward towards Tuckerman's Ravine in the White Mountains of New Hampshire. There was very little conversation, maybe due to the difficulty of the climb for Brent or because all that was needed that day was the quiet companionship they shared. Each one deep in their own thoughts or past memoires shared with his friend and her husband.

N

Widowhood: A year later? So what is new? There is no magic in this time frame. Whoever came up with this archaic notion must never had endured losing a spouse. Brent's advice to widowed friends: Do what you have to do in your own time frame, not what someone else or custom put on you. Sell the house? Move away? Travel! Develop new relationships, find new interests, and continue to educate yourself.

Expect unexpected comments, such as when walking down the street a complete stranger may admonish you to "SMILE." Or a coworker saying: "Are you going to stay here forever?" Or translated into: "Don't vegetate here, go get a life!"

Chapter 12

Epilogue

Steve and Brent did not have any children. Not that they did not want any, but because of what he knew, more than Brent did, of the uncertainty of his future.

In 1976, Brent married Paul C. Schulz, a Realtor in St. Petersburg, Florida. They have a son Paul D. Schulz who was born in 1983.

Paul was eagerly received as a son-in-law by Steve's parents, and young Paul was eagerly received as a grandson. Many visits and holiday gifts were exchanged between families until Mother Martin's death in 2010. Dad Martin had passed away in 1985; and both parents and their son are together in the same cemetery in New Hampshire.

Over the years many fond memories remain of the visits from Florida to New Hampshire. One of these is the visit that included Paul, Paul D.(at about nine months old) and Brent's second mother-in-law, Adele Schulz.

One evening Brent observed her father-in-law leaning over baby Paul's playpen, as he intently studied the little boy. She could only imagine his thoughts, as to his relationship to this child, not his son's child.

Dad Martin and Paul went out to lunch at a local restaurant, where upon, he introduced Paul as his son-in-law. He had come a long way from the early years of his grief.

Another poignant memory of that visit was from one warm New Hampshire summer evening. Brent observed her two mothers-in-law companionly sitting together, and she could hear the soft tone of their voices as they conversed. Brent felt so blessed to have these two wonderful women in her life; and to have been given love, the greatest gift of all, from their individual sons.

The Last Letter From Brent

Chapter 13

The Last Letter

June 18, 2018
St. Petersburg, Florida

My Dearest Steve,

This is probably my last letter to you. It has been almost 50 years since we have last written letters to each other. And, what letters they were. It seems that most of the five years from when we met; to the day I knew you would not be coming home to me, we communicated through letters written from our various schools, and your tour of duty in the Marine Corps. Of those five years, we only lived under the same roof for a little over two years.

Recently I have read every one of the 460 letters written between us, from the spring of 1963 to the fall of 1968. The first letters involved our dating, and escalated to the plans for our future home and life together. Then they started again from your Officers Training School in Quantico, Virginia in 1966; and again in 1968 from your tour in Vietnam.

You wrote the most beautiful letters, and in your perfect penmanship; which must have been passed on to you from your mother's artistic leaning. She was the one who created the beautiful artistic tribute to you for the books donated to the local library, in your memory.

How do I put into my words the letters from Vietnam from you. Your dedication to duty, your pride in the Marine Corps, your love for your country, your love for family, our love; and the respect you expressed for our marriage.

I will never forget the day we left you at the airport, as you left for Vietnam. You hugged us all. As you squared your shoulders, I saw your resolve, as you were a United States Marine answering the call of your country. Our eyes met as you walked away, I said your name, but you had gone. Oh, how I wanted just one more embrace.

Over the ensuing years; your parents, my parents, a six year old niece, aunts, uncles, cousins, and friends have passed away; but, I have never cried as many tears as I have cried over losing you.

My first love, my husband. Your Brent.

Acknowledgements

N

May I extend my sincere thanks and appreciation to the following people in my life, who humored me, offered advice, and even shared some tears with me as they read through the original manuscript leading to this book.

To the sisters, Betty Spongberg Keister and Jane Spongberg Walsh: The memory of both of you spending a whole weekend with me; pouring over the pages, making suggestions, and giving encouragement, will always be a most fond memory.

To Richard Wakefield, who expressed after reading the first chapters, that he wished to read the completed manuscript when it was done. Later, he would drive 26 miles round trip, to insist that I share the manuscript with a published author and editor he knew.

Two high school teachers, unknown to each other: Chet Borokowski, North Branford, Connecticut and Greg Denson, Hudson, Massachusetts. Your similar words: "This is history, and I want my students to read it." Wow, just wow!

To Kate Young Wilder, Author of "The House Where The Hardest Things Happened." Your expertise in writing, and your heartfelt interest in this endeavor, kept it moving forward.

Last but not least: To my son Paul D. Schulz: Your words were the first ones that kept me inspired: "Just keep writing, Mom. Just keep writing."

Addendum

N

Events In History: 1963 to 1968. Many things taken for granted today, were developed in these five years; as well as the happenings of national and world events.

1963:

President John F. Kennedy died on November 22, having been shot in Dallas, Texas.

Lyndon Johnson, Vice President, became President of the United States.

Martin Luther Kind, Jr. delivered his "I Have a Dream" Speech.

The average income per year was $5,807.00

Five digit zip codes were introduced July 1,1963

1964:

The Civil Rights Act of 1964 was signed into law.

Beatlemania occurred as The Beatles, a British singing group released: "I Want To Hold Your Hand," and "All My Loving."

The average cost of a new car was $3,500.00. A little over half the average income per year of $6,000.00.

The Tonkin Gulf Resolution gave the U.S. President Lyndon B. Johnson authorization, without a Formal declaration of war by congress, for the use of conventional military force in S.E. Asia.

1965:

Miniskirts appeared in London!

The Voting Rights Act becomes law giving African Americans the right to vote.

The average income per year was $6,450.00

Hypertext concept to be developed to be used for webpages on the Internet.

The respirator now to be used in place of the Iron Lung for assisting in breathing

1966:

The U.S. has nearly 500,000 troops in Vietnam.

Pampers produce the first disposable diaper.

Color television sets arrive on the scene.

The average income per year $6900.00

1967:

The world's first heart transplant by Dr. C. N. Barnard in South Africa.

The first automatic teller machine invented.

The first Super Bowl played between Green Bay Packers and the Kansas City Chiefs.

The first Boeing 737 takes flight.

The average income per year $7,300.00

1968:

Assassination of Martin Luther King, Jr.

McDonald's first Big Mac on sale for $.49.

Telephone emergency service 911 is started.

The tragedy of the My Lai massacre in Vietnam.

The first named Apollo mission.

Air bags in automobiles invented.

The average income per year $7,850.00

The average cost of a new car $2,822.00

According to the National Archives there were 58,220 U.S. Military casualties by the end of the

Vietnam War. Fifty-eight thousand, two hundred and twenty American Families suffered a loss!

(1971, The 26th Amendment: voting age changed to 18 as a response to debate on the Vietnam War.)

The Author

The author of "Only Five Years" is from Center Tuftonboro, a small town in New Hampshire. Life's events beckoned her to St. Petersburg, Florida where she has lived most of her adult life. Upon graduating from U.S.F. she worked for 26 years as a school teacher.

The preservation of the sentiments and history captured in the communications between Steven W. Martin, Captain U.S.M.C.R. and her, prompted the writing of this book. You are invited to join Steven and Brent on their journey.

Sincerely, Brent.

.

Made in the USA
Columbia, SC
24 October 2020